A GUIDE TO BRITISH MEDIEVAL SEALS

A GUIDE TO BRITISH MEDIEVAL SEALS

P.D.A. HARVEY AND ANDREW McGUINNESS

THE BRITISH LIBRARY
AND
PUBLIC RECORD OFFICE

First published 1996 jointly by
The British Library, Great Russell Street, London WC1 and
Public Record Office, Chancery Lane, London WC2

Cataloguing in Publication Data
A CIP Record is available from The British Library

ISBN 0 7123 0410 X

Design by John Mitchell
Typset in Monotype Sabon by August Filmsetting, Haydock, St Helens
Printed in England by Henry Ling at the Dorset Press, Dorchester

CONTENTS

ACKNOWLEDGMENTS

We are grateful to the following scholars who, having read all or part of our draft text, made valuable comments and suggestions, in several cases let us see their own unpublished work, and saved us from many errors – any in the final text are no one's fault but our own: Mr M.A.F. Borrie, Professor P.R. Coss, Dr D. Crook, Mr J.A. Goodall, Mr T.A. Heslop, Professor G.H. Martin, Professor M.C. Prestwich and, especially, Professor A.A.M. Duncan, but for whose generous help the Scottish aspects of the work would be much the poorer. We are grateful too to Dr P.A. Brand, Mr P. Walne, Miss R. Watson and the Revd Dr D.H. Williams, who have assisted us on particular points. We would also add our very special thanks to Janice Campbell and Yvonne Harvey for their support and help throughout.

P.D.A.H.

A.F.McG.

NOTES

1 The legends on seals are quoted with the use of capital letters normalised and, usually, with abbreviations expanded.

2 Places are identified by reference to the historic counties throughout Britain.

3 If no reference is given to a seal mentioned in the text it can be found in either W. de G. Birch, *Catalogue of Seals in the Department of Manuscripts in the British Museum* (London, 6v., 1887–1900), or J.H. Stevenson and M. Wood, *Scottish Heraldic Seals: Royal, Official, Ecclesiastical, Collegiate, Burghal, Personal* (privately printed, 3v., 1940).

4 The following abbreviations are used in the footnotes:

B.L.	British Library
D.C.D.	Dean and Chapter of Durham
Ellis	R.H. Ellis, *Catalogue of Seals in the Public Record Office* (London, 3v., 1978–86)
Hunter Blair	C. Hunter Blair, 'Durham Seals', in *Archaeologia Aeliana*, 3rd ser., vols 7–9 (1911–13), 11–16 (1914–19)
P.R.O.	Public Record Office

1 INTRODUCTION

SEALS AND THEIR EARLY HISTORY IN BRITAIN

The seal is a device for authenticating documents. Attached to the parchment or paper is the impression, in some relatively soft material, made by an engraved matrix that in principle is the personal property of its user, the person accepting responsibility for what the document says. Either the matrix, also known as the die, or the impression may be called a seal – which is meant depends on the context.

In medieval Britain sealing was for some three hundred years the way almost all documents were authenticated. Before the late eleventh century, however, the most solemn grants of lands and rights in England bore no seal but proclaimed their authority through their stately script and format and

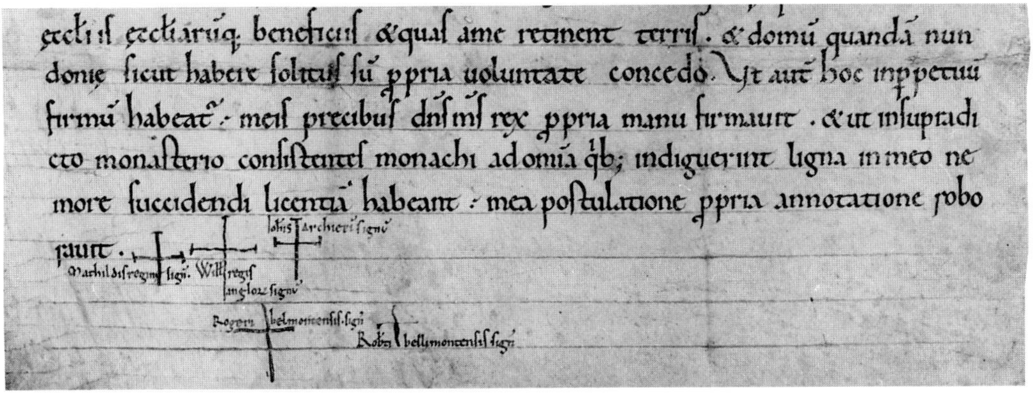

1 Document attested with crosses, 1068–76
Grant by Waleran of property at Bures St Mary, Suffolk, to St Stephen's Abbey, Caen, attested by the king and others in traditional form with crosses. Here, in Norman style, the crosses are autograph and the signatory's name has been added beside each – William I in the centre of the top row, with Queen Matilda on the left and John of Bayeux, bishop of Rouen, on the right, and with Roger and Robert de Beaumont below.
British Library, Additional Charter 75503

Fig 1 the names of their numerous eminent witnesses, each accompanied by the sign of the cross – some ecclesiastical documents still took this form throughout the twelfth century. The crosses, which might occasionally be autograph, were held to have sacred significance, invoking divine authority and protection for the transaction, whereas a seal might be seen as having only secular, legal, standing; some early-twelfth-century charters bore both, and later in the century a chronicler at Ramsey Abbey contrasted the duplicity of his own age, which used seals, with the open honesty of the tenth century, which did not.[1] Authentication by writing one's own name in one's own hand – the sign manual – was used by Edward III in 1362 probably simply because this was already the custom of the king of Castile, to whom he was writing, and here the autograph confirmed but did not replace the king's seal.[2] However, the practice spread rapidly in England in the late fourteenth and early fifteenth centuries, and other precursors can be found. Thus in 1298 the newly elected Master of the Gilbertine Order, having read out his profession of obedience to the bishop of Lincoln, offered the document at the altar and 'wrote at the bottom in his own hand'.[3] In 1330, at a time of political crisis, Edward III told the pope that letters on which he wrote 'Pater sancte' – Holy Father – in his own hand were the ones to be believed and acted upon.[4] But even in the fifteenth century, when the sign manual was in common use, seals were still used on all formal documents – and, on some highly formal occasions, authentication by actual or vestigial sealing survives in Britain to this day.

These same seals might, of course, serve other purposes too. At New Romney, Kent, by-laws current in the fourteenth century required anyone suspected of acquiring goods illicitly to set his seal on them in front of witnesses before going to find evidence that he came by them lawfully.[5] An impression of the pope's seal, placed at the top of the tower of St Albans Abbey, twice failed to stop it being struck by lightning in the mid-thirteenth century.[6] In this book we are concerned only with the seals intended primarily for documents, but the word seal is applied also to some other impressed designs from the middle ages, most notably in England and Wales to the cloth seals and woolsack seals, pieces of lead stamped with dies held by royal officials, that under statutes of 1353 and 1354 were attached to cloth for sale or to wool for export to show that tax had been paid. At Monmouth in 1380 we find a cloth seal being used to seal a document.[7] Similarities between these lead seals, document seals and contemporary coins in their design, and in the origin and manufacture of their dies, have as yet been only partly explored; the legend – inscription – around the edge of most kinds of seal is clearly related to those on coins, which like those on seals normally begin with a cross. Seals can properly be seen in the broad context of these and

[1] M.T. Clanchy, *From Memory to Written Record* (2nd edn, Oxford, 1993), p.311; W.D. Macray (ed.), *Chronicon abbatiae Ramesiensis* (Rolls Series; 1886), p.65.

[2] P. Chaplais, *English Royal Documents: King John – Henry VI* (Oxford, 1971), p.71.

[3] R.M.T. Hill (ed.), *The Rolls and Register of Bishop Oliver Sutton, 1280–1299* (Lincoln Record Society; 7v., 1948–75), i, p.233.

[4] C.G. Crump, 'The Arrest of Roger Mortimer and Queen Isabel', *English Historical Review*, 26 (1911), pp.331–2.

[5] K.M.E. Murray (ed.), *Register of Daniel Rough, Common Clerk of Romney, 1353–1380* (Kent Archaeological Society, Records Branch, vol.16; 1945), p.21.

[6] H.T. Riley (ed.), *Gesta abbatum monasterii sancti Albani* (Rolls Series; 3v., 1867–9), i, p.313.

[7] B.L. Additional Charter 55247.

other relics of replicated design from medieval Britain, among them jettons (counters used in accounting), pilgrim badges, stamped tiles and moulds used in baking.

The earliest English documents known to be authenticated by attached seals are writs – letters – of Edward the Confessor (1042–66) and this may well have been his own innovation in royal administrative practice, perhaps, in moving away from the documents with crosses, marking a new, more secular approach;[8] the earliest known from Scotland bears the seal of Duncan II in 1093–4. But this is not to say there were no seals in Anglo-Saxon England, though how many people owned them and how they were used is not at all clear. Five

2 Bishop Aethelwold, ninth century
Matrix and impression of a seal bearing the name of Bishop Aethelwold, probably bishop of East Anglia. The copper-alloy matrix, 7.0 cm. high, is decorated with animal heads which originally had garnets as eyes; it was found at Eye, Suffolk, in the early nineteenth century. The seal design, 3.2 cm. across, is strikingly like certain contemporary coins of Canterbury.

The seal is 3.2 cm across (enlarged).
British Museum, Department of Medieval and Later Antiquities, Seal-Die no.1

seal-dies survive from before the Norman Conquest; the earliest belonged to Bishop Aethelwold, probably the East Anglian bishop of the mid-ninth century, and they are all alike in making a circular impression, less than 5 centimetres across, and in including the owner's name. A similar seal, used by Wilton Abbey down to its dissolution, bore the name of its founder, Edith, who died in 984, and seals in the same style that were used by six other monasteries in the twelfth century may also be of pre-Conquest origin.[9] King

Fig 2

Fig 3

[8] B. Bedos-Rezak, 'The King Enthroned, a New Theme in Anglo-Saxon Royal Iconography', in J.T. Rosenthal (ed.), *Kings and Kingship* (Binghamton, 1986), pp.61–2.

[9] T.A. Heslop, 'English Seals from the Mid Ninth Century to 1100', *Journal of the British Archaeological Association*, 133 (1980), pp.2–7.

3 Wilton Abbey, tenth century
Though this was used as the abbey's seal until the sixteenth century, it bears the name of Edith, the founder, and was probably her personal seal; she died in 984. It shows her raising one hand in benediction and holding a book in the other. This impression, on a document of 1372, bears the marks of an ornamental handle, similar to other early matrices.
4.2 cm (actual size).
British Library, Harley Charter 45 A.36

Alfred in the late ninth century wrote of the authority implied by a lord's letter and seal, and in an early-eleventh-century dialogue for teaching Latin a pilgrim going to Rome asks some senior person for assistance in the form of 'a seal engraved with your name and a letter, so that in your name we may be helped and sustained by all'; the reply was that 'you ought to have my seal with a letter – I will not refuse you'. These passages imply that the seal had an authority independent of the letter, and it may be that it was not attached but was carried separately to authenticate not the letter so much as the bearer. This occurred on the Continent and a double-sided leaden seal of Cenwulf, king of Mercia (796–821), may have served this purpose, for it has been suggested that it was never attached to a document.[10] It is interesting that of sixteen references in Domesday Book (1086) to seals – of Edward the Confessor, William I and Odo, bishop of Bayeux – only three refer to 'writ and seal' or 'writ with seal'; of the rest, five say that neither seal nor writ (or message) has been seen by way of authorisation, and all the others mention the seal alone as though it had quite separate, independent, authority.[11] The legends on two early-twelfth-century seals can be read as hinting at independent use: 'Thor me mittit amicis' (Thor sends me to a friend) on a design showing the owner, Thor Longus, a Berwickshire landowner, sitting with his sword, and 'Signo stigma crucis Gualtham mittit amicis' (on this seal Waltham sends to friends the mark of the Cross) on a seal of Waltham Abbey showing the Cross with two angels. Alternatively they can be seen as referring to letters that they closed.[12] Clearly the seal given to the early-eleventh-century pil-

[10] P. Chaplais, 'The Anglo-Saxon Chancery: from the Diploma to the Writ', *Journal of the Society of Archivists*, 3, no.4 (1966), pp.167–9; W.H. Stevenson (ed.), *Early Scholastic Colloquies* (Anecdota Oxoniensia, Medieval and Modern Series, 15; 1929), p.26.

[11] The references are given under 'Breve' and 'Sigillum' in *Libri censualis, vocati Domesday-Book, indices* (Record Commission, 1816).

[12] Heslop, 'English Seals', pp.15–16.

grim was not used to close the letter, to be broken when it was opened and read, for it was to serve on more than one occasion. However, probably before the twelfth century, as certainly later, seals might be used to close documents; they would show that the contents were genuine and had not been tampered with en route to the recipient, but, being destroyed on opening, they could not serve as permanent authentication.

4 Edward the Confessor, 1042–66
The earliest known two-sided seal, made to hang from the document on a cord or parchment strip. On both sides it shows the king enthroned, with sceptre and orb in the front, sceptre and sword on the back, and on both sides it calls him *basileus*, a title sometimes given to Anglo-Saxon kings in their charters. This cast, of the clearest and most complete of the three known impressions, shows how valuable casts can be, for since it was made the original seal has been lost. It was on a grant of 1053–7 to St-Denis Abbey, Paris.

7.5 cm (actual size).
British Library, Doubleday Casts A 3, 4

The sealed writs that we first meet in Edward the Confessor's reign may or may not have introduced to England permanent authentication by sealing. Certainly they were entirely new in bringing together elements from diverse sources. The seal's design, the king enthroned, is the same as the seals of contemporary German kings. These, however, were attached to the face of the document; the English royal seal was pendent, hanging on a cord or tag like the lead seals – *bullae* – used to authenticate letters by the popes and the Byzantine emperors. And like the *bullae* and like coins, but unlike any other contemporary seals, the English king's seal was two-sided, impressed with a design not only on the front, or obverse, but also on the back, the reverse – again the king enthroned, but with different regalia. In Scotland, Duncan II's

Fig 4
Fig 5

5 Duncan II, 1093–4
The earliest surviving seal of a king of Scotland, it is known from a single impression, detached from whatever document it once authenticated. The king's name is now lost from the legend, but is recorded in an eighteenth-century description. The design is probably copied from the equestrian side of the seal of William I or William II, but unlike theirs it is a single-sided seal.
About 5.5 cm (actual size).
British Library, Seal xlvii.2

seal showed him on horseback, like one side of the seals of both William I (1066–87) and William II (1087–1100), but it was a single-sided seal, with the back blank, and Alexander I (1107–24) was the first Scottish king whose seal was two-sided. Here we see a peculiarly English innovation copied in Scotland; and by and large the form and style of seals followed much the same course in Scotland and in England throughout the middle ages. However, in medieval Scotland, certainly in the Highlands and possibly in the Lowlands too, less use was made of written documents in private administration and property transactions than in England and Wales; this means that although we find seals of the same kinds in both kingdoms, the use of personal seals was less widespread in Scotland.

Fig 23

But it seems proper to treat British medieval seals as a whole. In significant ways they are different from Irish seals on one hand, Continental seals on the other. All the same, some distinctive national groups occur within Britain – the naively designed equestrian seals of twelfth-century Wales, for instance,[13] or the group of bishops' seals from thirteenth-century Scotland with three-quarter face figure. Nor, of course, were British seals necessarily different from those elsewhere – the seal made for William de Mandeville, earl of Essex, about 1180 was modelled on that of Philip of Alsace, count of Flanders, the second great seal of Robert I of Scotland (1306–29) was copied from those of contemporary French kings,[14] and small personal seals from northern France in the twelfth and thirteenth centuries are all but identical with those from England and Wales. After all, many archives in medieval Britain – royal, ecclesiastical, aristocratic – will have contained papal and other letters from the Continent bearing seals that may easily have directly influenced design. There was in fact much influence from abroad on British

[13] M.P. Siddons, 'Welsh Equestrian Seals', *National Library of Wales Journal*, 23 (1983–4), pp.292–318.

[14] T.A. Heslop, 'Seals as Evidence for Metalworking in England in the Later Twelfth Century', in S. Macready and F.H. Thompson (eds), *Art and Patronage in the English Romanesque* (Society of Antiquaries, Occasional Papers, new ser. 8; London, 1986), pp.52, 57; A.A.M. Duncan (ed.), *The Acts of Robert I, King of Scots 1306–1329* (Regesta Regum Scottorum, vol.5; Edinburgh, 1988), pp.183–5.

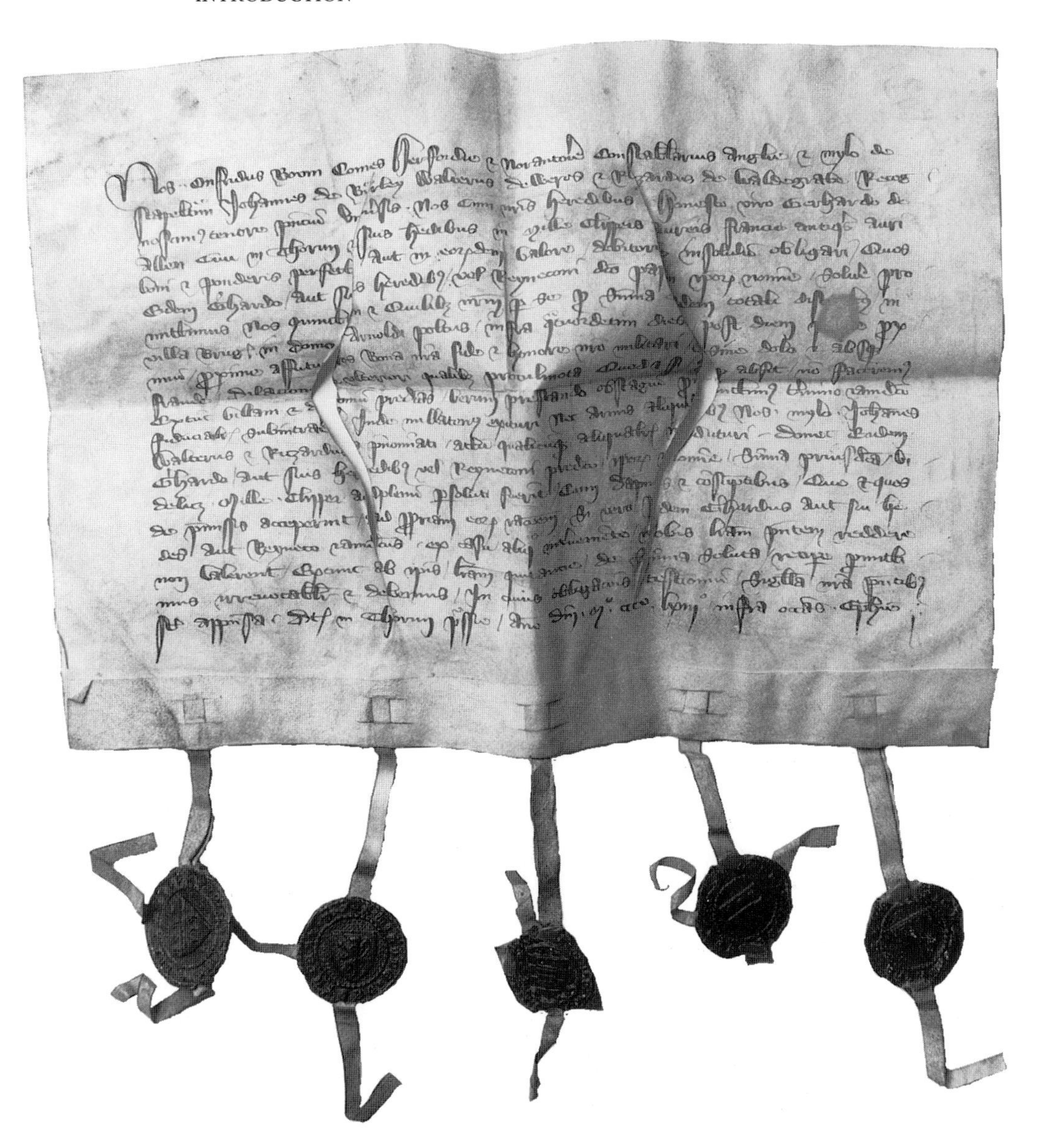

6 British and foreign seals, 1364
The earl of Northampton and four English knights sealed this document, dated at Torun, Poland. The damaged seal of John de Burley in the centre is of normal English style, but the others, coats of arms on a background of tiny quatrefoils, are quite unlike contemporary British seals and must have been made abroad, perhaps for this particular transaction.

Public Record Office, DL 25/1639

seals, and the design of – above all – ecclesiastical and town seals cannot be fully appreciated in isolation. Seals were surprisingly alike throughout medieval Britain but they were neither wholly homogeneous nor cut off from development elsewhere.

7 Matrix with ridge, 1461–2
In this common type of matrix, the ridge might be much lower, and a loop attached to the rim might replace the hole through the ridge. This is the official seal of Richard, duke of Gloucester, as admiral for Dorset and Somerset (see fig.34); it is made of copper alloy, gilt.

The seal is 7.6 cm across (actual size).
British Museum, Department of Medieval and Later Antiquities, Seal-Die no.27

THE SEAL-MATRIX

Bishop Aethelwold's seal in the ninth century was engraved at the base of a conical bronze mount, 7 centimetres high, ornamented with pierced arches and animals' heads. *Fig 2* Some other Anglo-Saxon seal-dies had a handle at the head of the engraving, more or less decorated; on some impressions of Edith's seal from Wilton Abbey the handle's acanthus ornament can be seen.[15] *Fig 3* Among later seal-dies there is some variety of shape, and their typology has never been investigated. Two forms of metal die are, however, particularly common. *Fig 7* One has either a raised ridge along the back, often with a loop on it, or a projecting tab at the top end, often looped and sometimes visible on the impression – or both. The other, which became more common in the fourteenth century, *Fig 8* has the seal engraved at the base of a conical handle, like Bishop Aethelwold's but much less ornate and straight-sided, usually hexagonal, in section with a loop at the top. The ridge or the handle provided a grip when the seal was being used; the loop was presumably to carry it on a chain or thong.[16] In the first half of the fourteenth century a few dies were made with the central part of the engraved design attached to a screw, *Fig 9* allowing it to be raised above the surrounding wording, the legend with the owner's name; this meant that the same die could be used

[15] Heslop, 'English Seals', pp.2, 4.

[16] A.B. Tonnochy, *Catalogue of British Seal-Dies in the British Museum* (London, 1952), pp.xxiv–xxv; S.E. Rigold, 'Two Common Species of Medieval Seal-Matrix', *Antiquaries Journal*, 57 (1977), pp.324–9.

8 Matrix with handle, 14th century
One of the commonest types of medieval seal matrix, six-sided and with three holes at the top, with or without a further loop above. This example, made of silver, is the seal of Ithel ap Bleddyn – a shield of arms couché, with helmet and crest, a maiden's head.

The seal is 2.6 cm across (enlarged).
British Museum, Department of Medieval and Later Antiquities, Seal-Die no.340

9 Matrix with screw-out centre, first half of fourteenth century
Only a few matrices of this sort are known. A screw allows the centre of the design to be raised above the legend round the edge (as shown in the centre), so that the seal can be used either with the legend (impression on the right) or without (impression on the left). This matrix is of silver. The seal bears the name of Henry le Callere – the cap-maker – and his merchant's mark which, as often, includes the outline of a shield and his initial, 'h'.

The seal is 2.4 cm across with the legend, 2.0 cm without (enlarged).
British Museum, Department of Medieval and Later Antiquities, Seal-Die no.341

Fig 30 to make an impression either with the legend or without.[17] A surviving signet ring has been identified as that of Richard I (1189–99),[18] and many of the counterseals that we find in the thirteenth century were probably made with signet rings. The counterseal was the more personal seal, usually quite small, impressed at the back of the wax to corroborate the owner's principal seal on the front – sometimes the back of a two-sided seal is called the counterseal, but it seems better to reserve the term for a separate seal, independently *Fig 10* applied. However, it was not until the fifteenth century that signet rings came into widespread use; this is shown by surviving examples as well as by

[17] H.S. Kingsford, 'Seal Matrices with Screw-Out Centres', *Antiquaries Journal*, 4 (1924), pp.249–56.

[18] P.E. Lasko, 'The Signet Ring of King Richard I of England', *Journal of the Society of Archivists*, 1, no.8 (1963), pp.333–5.

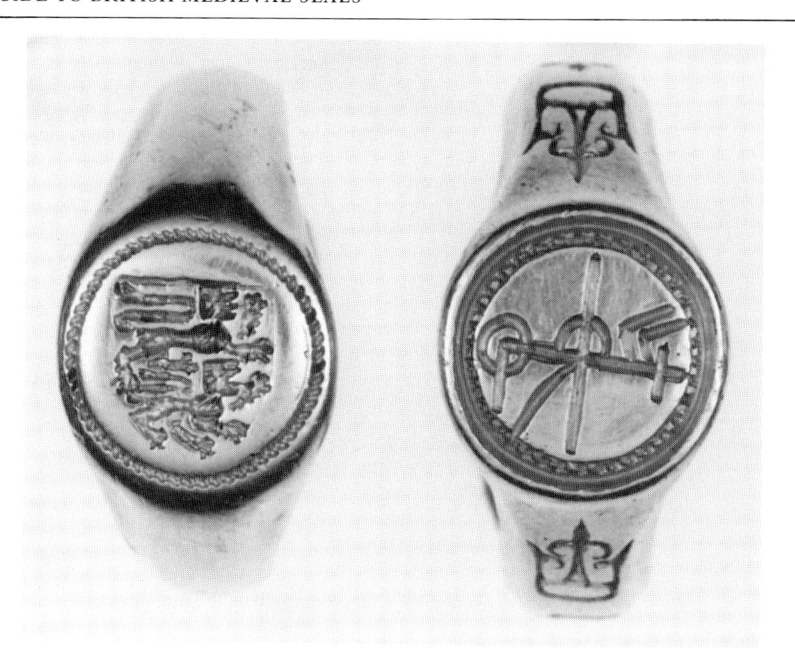

10 Two signet rings, fifteenth century
In the later middle ages signet rings were used for many kinds of personal seal. On the left is a shield of arms, two lions passant, and on the right a merchant's mark. Both rings are gold and were clearly made to order; those with a single initial or other impersonal design might be bought ready-made.
The seal on the left is 1.3 cm across, the seal on the right 1.4 cm (enlarged).
British Museum, Department of Medieval and Later Antiquities, Finger Rings nos 296, 356

seal impressions on which the shape of parts of the ring can often be seen, usually above and below the design.

From all these matrices impressions would be made simply by hand. The wax would be warmed to soften it – in an account of sealing a document in 1345 we are told how it was heated at the fire – then pressed carefully into the engraved design and the back of the wax moulded to shape; in the words of one late-medieval author, writing on astrology, 'planets stamped their impression on human beings like a seal on soft wax'.[19] The matrix would then be removed. Fingerprints of the person sealing often remain on the wax and late-medieval seals sometimes have adhering to them fragments of leaves, perhaps used to stop the wax sticking to the hand. However, if the seal was a two-sided one, direct manual pressure would be insufficient to secure an even impression. Instead, pressure might be applied either by a roller – like a rolling-pin – which we see being used in a fifteenth-century picture of the court of chancery, or by a seal-press, of which an example from about 1232 survives at Canterbury Cathedral. In either case the back of

Fig 11
Fig 12

[19] *Calendar of Patent Rolls 1345–8*, pp.4, 7; Heinrich von Langenstein, in R. Horrox (ed.), *The Black Death* (Manchester, 1994), p.103.

11 Chancery, mid-fifteenth century

On the right the great seal is being applied to a writ with a roller – the lugs of the matrix can be seen. On the table are writs ready to be sent out, and we see how routine writs – writs *de cursu* – bore the impression of only a portion of the great seal; this is how they could be sealed without a seal-press. The picture is one of four showing the king's courts at Westminster; they were drawn to illustrate a collection of law reports, but the rest of the book is lost.

Library of the Inner Temple

the matrix would have to be flat. To ensure that the two sides of the seal exactly coincided, from two to four lugs projected from each matrix, with holes on one, pegs on the other; these would hold the matrices in position during sealing, and traces of these lugs sometimes appear on the seal impressions. Applying pressure by screws through the holes in the lugs may have been an alternative to a seal-press.[20] From the late twelfth to the mid-thirteenth century a few English monasteries had peculiarly elaborate seals made, where the design on one or both sides was built up from two matrices. The seal of about 1258 from Southwick Priory in Hampshire is an example. First the wax would be impressed with the single obverse matrix, showing the Virgin and Child in an architectural setting, and with the first of the reverse matrices, quite plain apart from the figure of Christ above and the Annunciation below. This matrix would then be removed from the reverse and replaced with a further thin layer of wax, on which the second reverse matrix was impressed, an elaborate architectural surround, which could be cut through to reveal the figures below. This technique gave parts of the

Fig 13

Fig 14

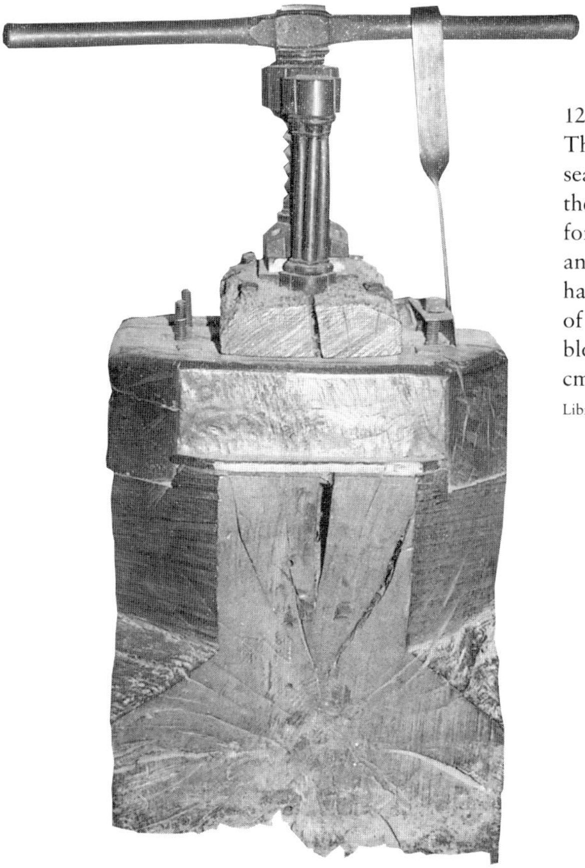

12 Seal-press, thirteenth century
This press, for impressing wax with a two-sided seal, is at Canterbury Cathedral. It exactly fits the new and elaborate seal that was engraved for the cathedral priory in 1232 or just before, and was probably made at the same time. The handle is iron, but the rest of the press is made of copper alloy and it is mounted on an oak block. The columns on each side are about 19 cm. high.
Library of Canterbury Cathedral

[20] Duncan (ed.), *Acts of Robert I*, p.196.

impression added depth, even an effect of undercutting.[21]

Most medieval seal-matrices were made of metal. A very few were engraved in gold: the so-called golden great seal of Henry IV, Henry V and Henry VI may in fact have been silver-gilt,[22] but there are surviving gold signet rings and some other seals of great persons were almost certainly of gold. The usual material for the best matrices was silver, but much more commonly used were alloys of copper variously termed brass, bronze or latten. In the thirteenth century the simplest designs of seal were often

Fig 28

13 Matrix with lugs and pegs, fourteenth century
To align correctly the two faces of a two-sided seal its matrices were made with two, three or four projecting lugs, pierced with holes into which pegs fitted. This example is the seal of Inchaffray Abbey, Perthshire, made of copper alloy. In front is a church with the figure of St John the Evangelist, the abbey's patron, and on the back his symbol of the eagle. Where, as here, there was a lug at top or bottom of the matrix the design would have to be slanted if the seal was attached to a tag.
The seal is 6.9 cm across (reduced).
British Museum, Department of Medieval and Later Antiquities, Seal-Die no.938

engraved on lead with ridge and loop at the back. Matrices are also known engraved in ivory, jet and soapstone.

In all these cases there seems to be no simple correlation between the design of a seal impression and the material or form of the matrix, though this may emerge from further research; at present one can only make the obvious comment that the most elaborate, finely detailed designs are the most likely to have been engraved on precious metal. However, one material used for the matrices of personal seals can usually be identified from the

[21] The process is described by F. Madden, 'Remarks on the Matrix of the Seal of Boxgrave Priory, in Sussex', *Archaeologia*, 27 (1838), pp.375–80.

[22] H. Jenkinson, 'A New Great Seal of Henry V', *Antiquaries Journal*, 18 (1938), pp.383–4.

impression: the engraved gem, recognisable by its particular style of engraving and, often, by its design. The paste, or semi-precious stone such as cornelian, jasper or onyx, would be engraved, like other seal-dies, in intaglio, that is, so that on the impression the design stands up in relief. Sometimes the gem formed the entire engraved surface of the die and would

14 Three-part matrix, mid-thirteenth century
A few English monasteries had seals built up from more than two matrices. Southwick Priory, Hampshire, used this triple matrix of copper alloy. The front of the seal was made with the single matrix on the right, showing a church with Virgin and Child; the back was impressed first with the matrix in the centre, showing Christ above and the Annunciation below, then, after a further thin layer of wax was added, with the matrix on the left, another church design through which openings could be cut in the wax to reveal the figures below. There may originally have been a fourth part of the matrix to add a legend around the rim.

The seal is 7.0 cm across (reduced).
Hampshire Record Office, 153M88/1

include any wording; sometimes the legend would be on a surround of other material. Some of the gems used as seals were set in signet rings – Richard I's ring comprises a gem in a gold setting engraved with the legend – and others were not, though by the fifteenth century gems mostly appear only in rings. Occasionally gems are inset into the matrix of a larger engraved seal. The gems might date from classical antiquity, but most were probably later copies and even when the matrix survives it can be impossibly difficult to determine its age. Designs included classical busts and pastoral scenes, but also contemporary Christian motifs such as the Cross, the Lamb of God, angels and saints. Some stones and some of their engraved designs were held

Fig 30

Fig 15

to have particular medical or magical properties.[23]

In about 1150 the abbot of St Albans, suspecting his monks of conspiring against him, discovered an incomplete seal-die on the workbench of Anketil, monk, 'matchless goldsmith' and former warden of the mint to the king of Denmark.[24] Throughout the middle ages it was goldsmiths who engraved the finest, most elaborate, seals. In 1218 Walter de Ripa, goldsmith, was paid £5.6s.8d. for the first great seal of Henry III, and from then on, English royal accounts record the names of a number of those who produced seals for the

15 Engraved gems in seals, 13th and early 14th centuries
Examples of seals made from engraved gems, set with legend engraved around the mount. All three are impressions from surviving matrices that are not signet rings. The gem on the right is plasma, and the angel was engraved in the fifth century; the other two are jasper and the engraving is medieval, as the subjects clearly show. The gem in the centre is set in gold, the other two in silver. All three legends are mottoes that do not name the seal's owner.

Left 2.7 cm, centre 2.5 × 2.2 cm, right 2.7 × 2.1 cm (enlarged).
British Museum, Department of Medieval and Later Antiquities, Seal-Dies nos 704, 705, 707

Crown; some are specifically called the king's engravers and most or all worked in London.[25] Unusual evidence of provincial seal-making is the early-thirteenth-century seal-matrix of the city of Exeter, which has its maker's name, Luke – 'Lucas me fecit' – engraved on the handle; from their similar style he is thought to have been responsible also for the seals of two hospitals at Exeter and of the borough of Taunton.[26] But fine engraving played no part in the manufacture of most medieval seals, and few can in fact have been goldsmiths' work. Craftsmen called seal-maker (*sigillarius*) start to appear in the late thirteenth century and a list, in 1422, of 'the names of all

[23] Tonnochy, *Catalogue of British Seal-Dies*, pp.xviii–xxi; G. Henderson, 'Romance and Politics on some Medieval English Seals', *Art History*, 1 (1978), p.27.

[24] Riley (ed.), *Gesta abbatum*, i, pp.84, 86, 107–8.

[25] H.S. Kingsford, 'Some Medieval Seal-Engravers', *Archaeological Journal*, 97 (1940), pp.158–80.

[26] ibid., pp.156–8.

the crafts exercised in London from of old and still continuing' has a separate entry for seal-engravers.[27] In 1380 two men sealed a forged will 'with a seal marked with an H, which they had bought at Paul's Gate' – by the late fourteenth century in London, and doubtless elsewhere, seals could be bought over the counter.[28] Matrices have been found with spaces left blank for the wording: the name or motto would be added on the customer's orders when the seal was bought.[29] Stone moulds survive for casting the backs of matrices, and the principal element of the design was sometimes cast, not engraved.[30] Lettering might be entered on the die from punches, and their outlines between one letter and the next can sometimes be seen on seal-impressions.[31] These techniques need not have been peculiar to lesser seals: goldsmiths used punches as well as graving tools for both the design and the lettering, and it seems likely that, when a royal seal needed extensive alteration, instead of re-engraving the old matrix a new one might be made by casting.[32]

Many of these questions about the origin and manufacture of seal-matrices could be answered by detailed research on seal-impressions as well as on the matrices themselves, and in work on the seals of Richard of Bury, bishop of Durham (1333–45) T.A. Heslop has opened the way to new standards of investigation. Sometimes it is clear that seals on related documents are the work of a single engraver, and in a few cases a single fine craftsman has been identified in a series of seals, as Luke at Exeter, or the goldsmith, presumably of London, who engraved seals for both the city of Carlisle and Southwick Priory, Hampshire, in the mid-thirteenth century, or another unknown goldsmith of the 1330s who produced three seals for Richard of Bury and one for John of Kirkby, bishop of Carlisle.[33] There is still much to be learned of the way seal designs originated, were copied and migrated. Some close similarities in design have been noted – the twelfth-century chapter seals of Hereford and Llandaff, for instance, or a group of bishops' seals from early-thirteenth-century Scotland.[34] Some more distant connections can be found. The same rhyming couplet appears on the seals of Milton Abbey in Dorset and Arbroath Abbey in Angus, the eagle of St John the

[27] E.M. Veale, 'Craftsmen and the Economy of London in the Fourteenth Century', in A.E.J. Hollaender and W. Kellaway (eds), *Studies in London History* (London, 1969), pp.139–41.

[28] I.J. Leadam and J.F. Baldwin (eds), *Select Cases before the King's Council 1243–1482* (Selden Society, vol.35; 1918), p.73.

[29] J. Alexander and P. Binski (eds), *Age of Chivalry: Art in Plantagenet England 1200–1400* (London; 1987), p.398.

[30] J. Blair and N. Ramsay (eds), *English Medieval Industries: Craftsmen, Techniques, Products* (London, 1991), pp.xxvi, 119–20.

[31] e.g. P.R.O. DL 25/1234 (first seal).

[32] Jenkinson, 'New Great Seal', p.384; Blair and Ramsay (eds), *English Medieval Industries*, p.120.

[33] Alexander and Binski (eds), *Age of Chivalry*, p.400; T.A. Heslop, 'The Episcopal Seals of Richard of Bury', in N. Coldstream and P. Draper (eds), *Medieval Art and Architecture at Durham Cathedral* (British Archaeological Association, Conference Transactions, 3; 1980), p.156.

[34] D.H. Williams, *Catalogue of Seals in the National Museum of Wales* (Cardiff, in progress, 1993–), i, p.5; W.de G. Birch, *History of Scottish Seals* (Stirling, 2v., 1905–7), ii, p.32.

Evangelist and its surrounds are all but identical on the seals of Inchaffray Abbey in Perthshire and the borough of Kings Lynn. Seal-engravers might work in a limited area, but the seal impressions – and thus their designs – might travel far. We know practically nothing of regional styles or preferences in the design of seals, and very little of local centres of production. How far casting played a part in replicating designs, whether of royal seals or of any others, could be determined by minute examination of impressions and matrices. Further work on medieval exchequer and wardrobe records might give us the names of more of the craftsmen who made seals for the Crown. If much has been left vague in this account of seal-matrices it is because much has still to be discovered, not because it is undiscoverable.

Fig 13

MATERIAL AND MEANS OF ATTACHMENT

Seals in medieval Britain were always impressed in beeswax, to which in the later middle ages resin was added, and occasionally they contain fine hairs, presumably to strengthen the wax. A few particularly important documents issued by the pope and some other rulers either had the seal impressed on gold or else bore what was in effect a facsimile seal specially engraved in gold on each occasion; the only known British gold seal was attached by Henry VIII to his treaty with the king of France in 1527. The *bulla* of King Cenwulf of Mercia is the only lead seal known from medieval Britain, and wafer (a mixture of flour and gum) and shellac (sealing-wax) were not used in the middle ages. At first the wax was uncoloured; of the eighteen English royal seal-impressions surviving from before 1100 one is in brown wax and all the rest in white,[35] and uncoloured wax was often used in the twelfth century and sometimes even as late as the fourteenth. This is a pity, as seals without colouring are more friable and less likely to survive intact. The colouring was normally green (verdigris), red (vermilion) or brown which may sometimes result from the deterioration of one of the other colours. Other colours are found, but what appear at first sight to be black seals are nearly always very dark green or brown. Wax of two colours – often green and white – might be used to give a flecked or mottled effect, and occasionally the impression in one colour of wax would be surrounded and backed with another. Before the thirteenth century the impression was often coated in varnish, which on white or green seals can be seen as reddish-brown patches on the surface of the wax.

It is known that English offices of state systematically used different colours of wax for particular purposes and that the Scottish royal chancery varnished the seals on charters but not on other documents.[36] Otherwise, however, the chronology, distribution and use of the various colours in medieval seals are an unexplored topic, which might throw an interesting light on the processes of sealing and on the administrative practices of magnates, corporate bodies and individual lawyers or clerks. Where there is more than one seal on a document the wax is usually the same – but not

35 T.A.M. Bishop and P. Chaplais (eds), *Facsimiles of English Royal Writs to A.D. 1100 presented to Vivian Hunter Galbraith* (Oxford, 1957), pp.xix–xx.

36 Chaplais, *English Royal Documents*, p.15; Duncan (ed.), *Acts of Robert I*, p.196.

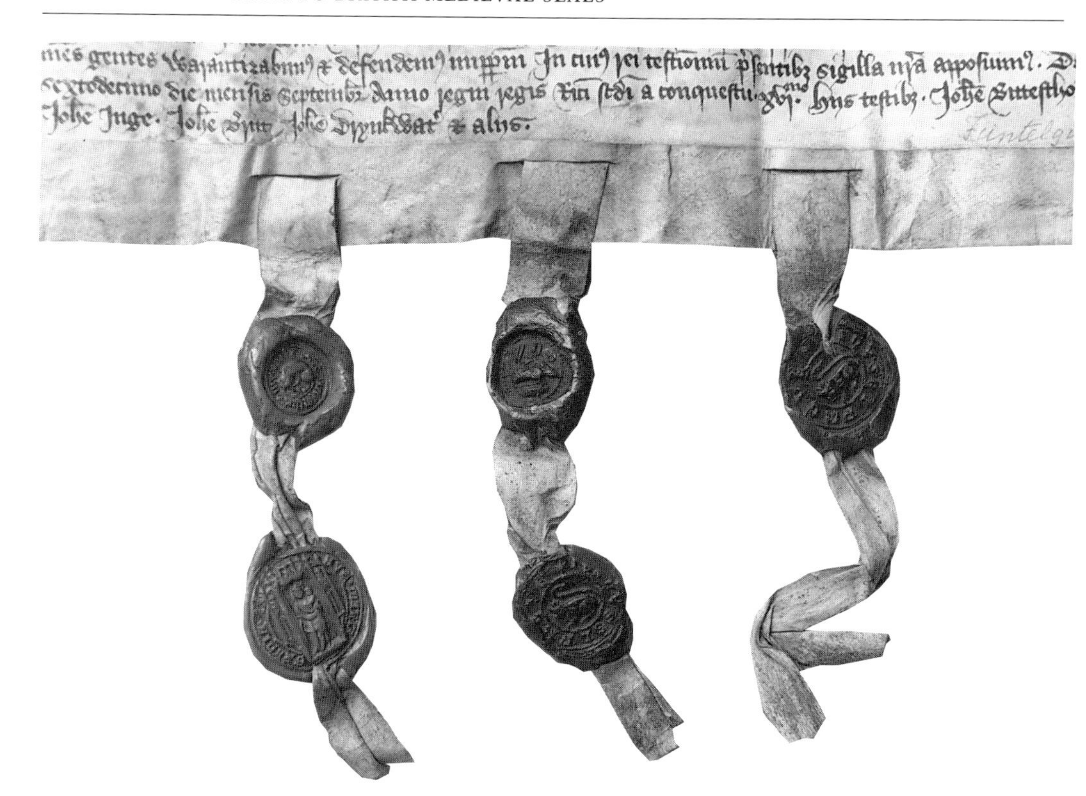

16 Seals on tags, 1392
Strips of parchment, threaded through the foot of the document and then sealed, are called tags. There might be more than one seal on each tag and sometimes a tag would be split – a double tag – with a seal on each half. Here on the centre (lower seal) and right-hand tags are two impressions of the same anonymous seal, serving as authentication by two of the document's signatories. The upper seal on the left-hand tag was used by Gilbert Stone and the legend, 'Gret wel Gibbe oure cat', may be a play on his name – Gib was a shortened form of Gilbert as well as a generic name for any cat.

Public Record Office, E 329/228

always. When the colour differs does this necessarily mean that sealing occurred at different times and places, like the late-medieval leases of Westminster Abbey's demesne lands that had the lessees' seals applied locally, the abbey's seal in chapter at Westminster?[37] In 1310 and 1319 we find the seal of Thomas, earl of Lancaster, impressed on wax of a distinctive shade of carmine-red.[38] Might a magnate use wax of a peculiar colour as an extra check on forgery – or even as a kind of brand-image, like his retainers' livery? Might a lesser individual also insist on always using the same colour wax for his or her seal?

There were three common ways of attaching the seal to the document.

[37] B. Harvey, *Westminster Abbey and its Estates in the Middle Ages* (Oxford, 1977), p.153.
[38] P.R.O. DL 25/960, 961.

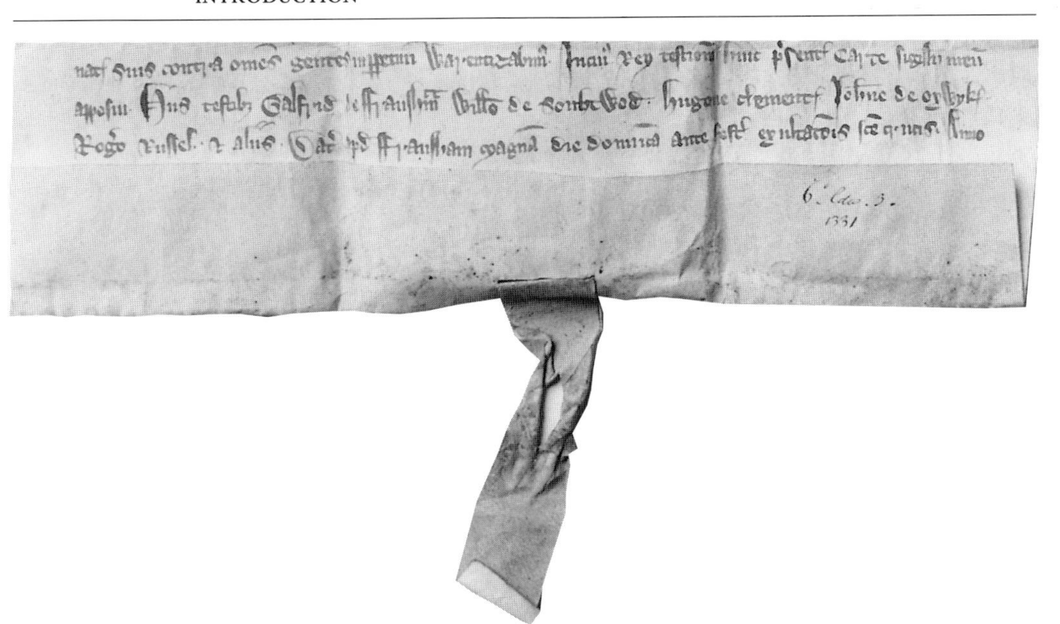

17 Tag prepared for sealing, 1332
The seal has been lost from this deed, showing how the tag was prepared for sealing: the two ends were passed through a vertical slit, making a gap in the parchment and giving the wax greater purchase. The wax would entirely cover this area, hiding all trace of this preparation.
Public Record Office, LR 14/573

One was to suspend it on a cord or woven band, or a thin strip of parchment known as a tag, that would pass through holes or slits at the bottom of the document, folded back for added strength. *Fig 16* The cord might be of silk or of linen or woollen thread; it might be plaited or woven; it might be of one colour or two. The tag might be cut from some scrap of used parchment, often the draft of the document itself; at the point on the tag where the seal was placed its ends were passed through a slit in the tag itself, twisting the parchment to give the wax greater purchase and to reduce risk of fissure. *Fig 17* On a few documents of the mid-fourteenth century the great seal of Scotland was attached to a tag that was threaded and tied with a cord.[39] The second method was to attach the seal to a strip of parchment nearly, but not quite, cut away from the bottom of the document; this strip is known as the tongue and below it was sometimes a much thinner strip, the tie, used notionally or actually to tie round the document and close it. *Fig 18* The third method of attachment was the applied seal: the wax was simply laid on the surface of the parchment – or of the wood, for this is how the tallies used as vouchers in accounting would be sealed. We know less of the ways seals were used to close documents – inevitably, since opening the document involved the destruction of the seal and, often, of the means of closure. However, we

[39] A.A.M. Duncan, 'The Regnal Year of David II', *Scottish Historical Review*, 68 (1989), p.111.

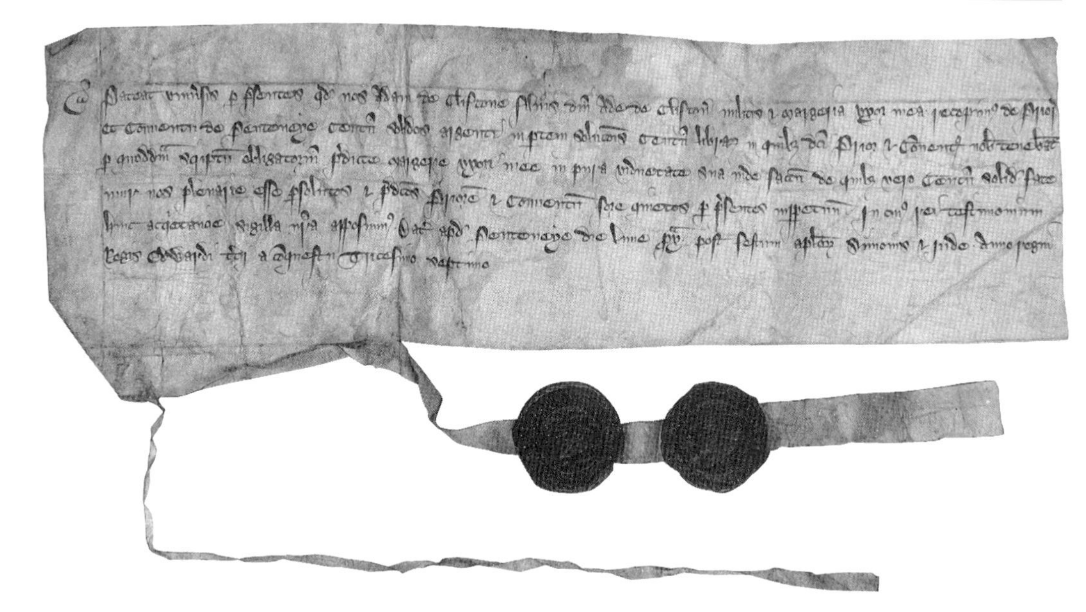

18 Seals on tongues, 1363
A strip of parchment nearly cut away from the foot of the document, then sealed, is called a tongue. On this example there are two seals, and below it is a thinner strip called the tie, that would be passed round the document if the seal was to be used to close it. The seals, both with shields of arms, are those of Adam de Clifton, knight, and his wife, Margery, but the surname and impaled arms on Margery's seal are those of her former husband, Richard de Bellhouse.
Public Record Office, LR 14/265

know several methods by which royal letters in fourteenth-century England and Scotland were closed by the seal, and a private letter of 1346 seems to have had the seal applied to the back across a parchment strip that was threaded through eight slits, closing the letter and bearing the address, 'To our very dear uncle the earl of Lancaster'.[40]

All three means of open attachment were used throughout the middle ages in Britain. Where a great many seals were attached to a document – and there might be fifty or more – tags or cords would be used; as we shall see, such documents provide a valuable snapshot of the seals that were in use by a particular group of people. Broadly speaking, however, the most important kinds of document had the seal on cord or tag, less important ones on tongue, and applied seals – the simplest but most precarious method – were restricted to writings of only temporary value. Medieval precedents can be found for impressing the seal through paper that remains covering the impression; this prevented the sealing material from sticking to the matrix and became very common later when wafer was used instead of wax – an

Fig 55

[40] Chaplais, *English Royal Documents*, pp.30–2, 37–8; Duncan (ed.), *Acts of Robert I*, pp.193–5; P.R.O. DL 25/985.

unusually early example is an agreement made at Newcastle-upon-Tyne in 1357 between two officials, the king's escheators.[41] It is much more common on small seals of the fourteenth and fifteenth centuries to find a twisted or plaited reed, or very thin strip of parchment, embedded in the wax around the impression. This served to protect or strengthen the seal.

Fig 19

19 Straw around a seal impression, 1479
The fragility of seals was a constant problem. One method used to strengthen a seal in the late middle ages was to press twisted straw into the wax around the impression. In this example the impression has been distorted by the straw ring and the design cannot now be identified.
1.2 × 1.0 cm (enlarged).
British Library, Egerton Charter 1375

The fragility of seals was in fact a recognised problem. An early-fourteenth-century inventory of Ramsey Abbey's muniments notes a few cases where seals are missing or broken, and so too, perhaps more systematically, does the Liber Ruber of Merton College, Oxford, a slightly earlier cartulary-like catalogue;[42] most of the documents listed at Merton College still survive there, and on a significant proportion of those with seals now broken or lost the damage had already occurred by the fourteenth century. To avoid these risks, seals were often given protective wrappings or bags. An outstanding collection of seal-bags comes from Canterbury Cathedral Priory: there the most important charters have their seals enclosed in bags of antique oriental silk that was probably cut from discarded vestments,[43] and this may have been the origin of the seal-bag of Chinese silk with gold brocade that was made at Holy Trinity Priory, Aldgate, London, for a document of between 1162 and 1170 sealed by Thomas Becket, archbishop of Canterbury. Most seal coverings are much simpler than this: bags of wool, linen or leather, or wrappings of cloth, paper or parchment held in place by hemp thread. They were not always effective: closely bound cloth would protect the seal from knocks but causes the wax to deteriorate, so that tight wrappings now often contain only the crumbled fragments of the seal.

Fig 20

[41] P.R.O. LR 14/1051.

[42] W.H. Hart and P.A. Lyons (eds), *Cartularium monasterii de Rameseia* (Rolls Series; 3v., 1884–93), i, pp.63–74; Merton College, muniments vol.1.1.

[43] G. Robinson and H. Urquhart, 'Seal Bags in the Treasury of the Cathedral Church of Canterbury', *Archaeologia*, 84 (1934), pp.163–211.

20 Medieval seal-bag of Chinese silk
This bag, made of a fragment of red silk with gold brocade, was used to protect the seal on a document belonging to Holy Trinity Priory, London. In the document Thomas Becket, archbishop of Canterbury, confirms the grant to the priory of the church of Bexley, Kent; it dates from 1162–70 but the bag may have been made later. In the Chinese design the three circles represent earth, air and water. Such an ornate seal-bag is unusual, but simpler protective coverings for medieval seals are not uncommon.
Public Record Office, E 40/4913

THE STUDY OF SEALS

The study of seals is called sigillography or sphragistics. Already in the fifteenth century their value as authenticating legal evidence of title began to blend with their value as heraldic and genealogical evidence and their still wider antiquarian interest. When Thomas of Elmham wrote his history of St Augustine's Abbey, Canterbury, at the beginning of the fifteenth century, he included not simply copies of the abbey's charters but facsimiles with careful drawings of the seals.[44] Interest in seals has gone hand in hand with the development of antiquarian studies from the sixteenth century onwards. The very first topic on which Francis Tate, secretary of the first English Society of Antiquaries, collected notes for a lecture to the Society was 'Of the Antiquity of seales &c'', and one delivered on 23 June 1591 was 'Of thoriginal of seling here in England with armes or otherwise'.[45] When, in 1638, Sir Christopher Hatton and three friends agreed to co-operate in work on antiquities, William Dugdale undertook to 'collect and coppy all armorial seales, with a breviate of ye deedes and ye true dimensions of ye seales'; probably a result of this was the magnificent volume of facsimiles of charters, with their

[44] M. Hunter, 'The Facsimiles in Thomas Elmham's History of St. Augustine's, Canterbury', *The Library*, 5th series 28 (1973), pp.215–20; A. Gransden, *Historical Writing in England* (London, 2v., 1974–82), ii, pp.350–4.

[45] B.L. Stowe MS. 1045, ff.6, 13.

Odo baiocensis eps. Lanfranco archiepo. & Hammoni uicecomiti. & omnib; cantuariensib; regis fidelib; salutē. Notum sit uobis. qđ ego O. baiocensis eps. & comes cantie. nostre matri que in honore scē trinitatis estructa est cantuariensi eccle: trado has quatuor dennas terre. uidelicet Lossenham. & Adalardendenā. & Blaccecotā. & Acdenā. a dono Lanfranco archiepō & omnib. successorib; ei pperpetuo usu possidendas. p redēptione domini mei Guilelmi regis anglorum. & mee. & eor quor salute specialit' iniunctu est michi pcurare. & p excābio xx & v. acrar terre que infra parcum meum de Wikeham continentur.

Odo b of baius. gret Landfranc arceb. 7 hæmonē scir gerefan. 7 ealle þoes kinges þegenas on cænt freondlice. Si eorl eallū cūđ. þ ic Odo b of baius. 7 eorl on cænt. ge ann ure moder þis xpes cirecean on cantware byrig. þas feower dene landes. þ is losenham. 7 Adalardan dene. 7 blaccecotan. 7 ac dena. Swa þ se larceow Landfranc 7 se arceb. 7 ealle his æfter gengan. hi heom ge agnian on ece yrfe. þis ic do for minnes laforder alysednesse Willelmes kinges. 7 for minre. 7 for þæra manna alysednesse. be þæra halu me is swiđelice gymene. 7 for ge hwyrfe fif 7 twentigra æcera landes; þa liggađ wiđ innan minū deor falde æt Wiccham.

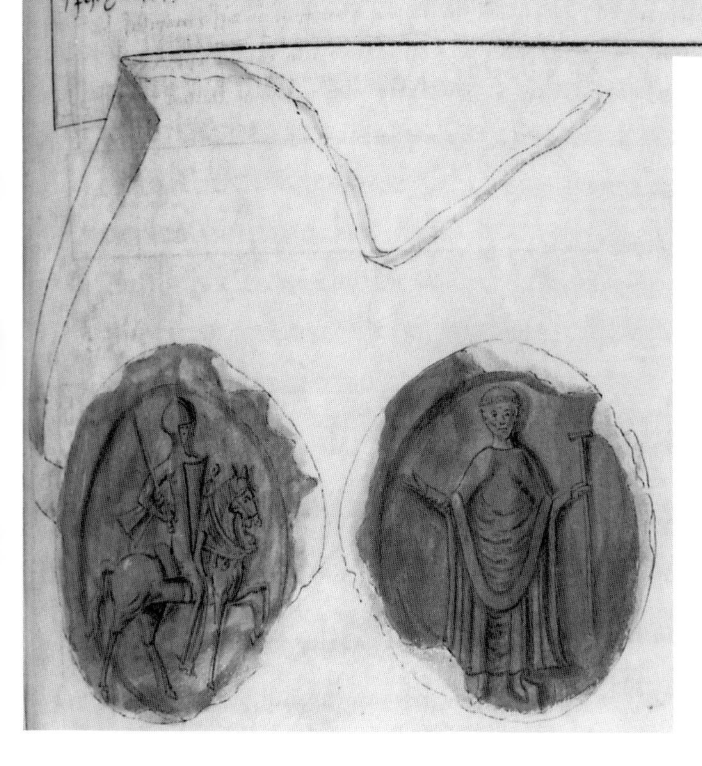

21 Drawing, 1641–2, of a document with the seal of Odo, bishop of Bayeux, 1071–82
This is our only record of Odo's seal – it is now lost from the charter copied here, and no other impression is known. Its design reflects his two roles – he was earl of Kent as well as bishop. Like casts, early drawings of seals can be important for the seal itself may be lost or damaged. This is from the Book of Seals made for Sir Christopher Hatton, which reproduced documents, with or without seals, in facsimile – note the difference in script between the Latin and Old English portions of this charter.

Northamptonshire Record Office, Finch Hatton MS. 170, f.92r

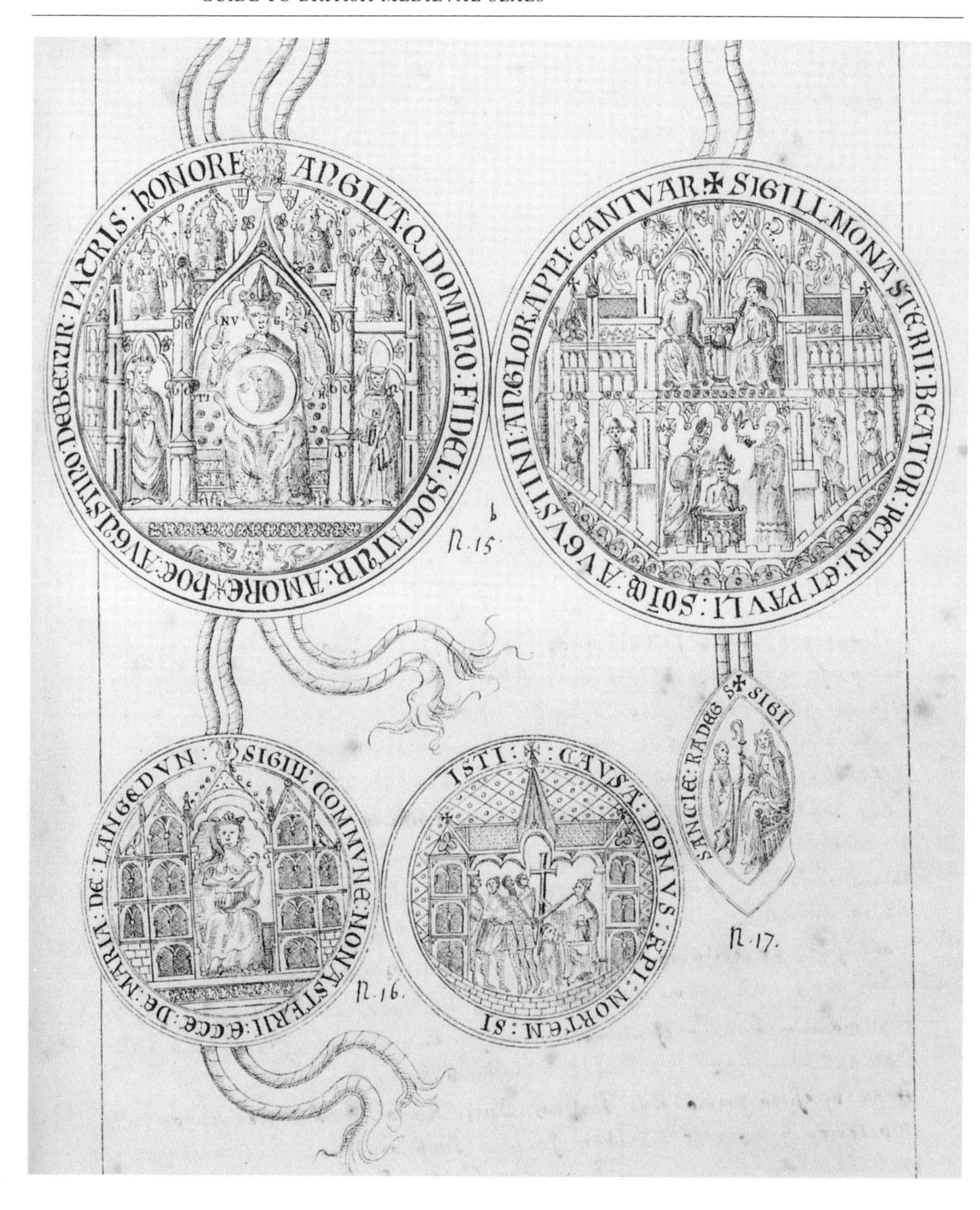

22 Drawings, eighteenth century, of thirteenth- and fourteenth-century monastic seals from Kent
Three contrasting seals: a magnificent fourteenth-century two-sided seal of St Augustine's Abbey, Canterbury, showing Augustine's baptism of King Aethelbert on the back, the smaller two-sided seal of Langdon Abbey, Kent, showing the martyrdom of Thomas Becket, and the simple pointed-oval seal of St Radegund's Abbey, near Dover. These carefully detailed drawings are from the unpublished treatise on seals, 'Aspilogia', by John Anstis, Garter King of Arms 1718–44.

British Library, Stowe MS. 665, f.82r

Fig 21 seals, known, significantly, in the seventeenth century as now, as the Book of Seals.[46] Dugdale himself introduced a short but valuable digression on seals into his *Antiquities of Warwickshire*, first published in 1656,[47] but the earliest published monograph on British medieval seals appeared in 1740: *A Dissertation on the Antiquity and Use of Seals in England*, by the Kentish historian John Lewis. In some thirty pages he discusses the introduction of seals to England and the way their ownership spread to all ranks of society. Though showing a proper scepticism he quotes a rhyme that tells how William the Conqueror sealed documents with his teeth –

> And in token that this Thing is sothe,
> I bite the white Wax with my fang Tothe,
> Before Meg, Maud, and Margerie,
> And my third Son Henry

– deriving perhaps from Thomas of Elmham's more convincing account of a grant to Castle Acre Priory, Norfolk, sealed by the earl of Lincoln with his teeth and witnessed by his wife Muriel, on which 'even now the toothmarks can be seen in the wax instead of a seal'.[48] A much more thorough and scholarly work than Lewis's, but unpublished, was written by John Anstis *Figs 22, 50, 51* the elder, Garter King of Arms from 1718 to 1744, and illustrated with over 750 careful drawings of English seals,[49] and in 1796 the Society of Antiquaries of London published engravings of some ninety Scottish seals, with historical notes by the archivist Thomas Astle, *An Account of the Seals of the* *Fig 46* *Kings, Royal Boroughs, and Magnates of Scotland.*

Lewis mentions 'the curious Collection of Seals of the Earls of Richmond, made by the learned Editor of the Register of that HONOWR' – that is Roger Gale, friend of William Stukeley – and, indeed, medieval seals were coming to be regarded as collectables, like cameos, medals or coins. In the nineteenth century collections came to include not only seals detached from their documents but also casts of other seals. Among particularly important collections of casts are those of the Society of Antiquaries of London and two acquired by the British Museum (now in the British Library), one presented by John Doubleday in 1837 and the other, mostly of Scottish seals, bought from Henry Laing in 1877. Casts are more valuable than may appear at first sight – *Figs 4, 23* the original seal may have been damaged or lost, giving the cast the status of primary evidence. Casts as well as original seals, whether on documents or detached, are included in the monumental *Catalogue of Seals in the Department of Manuscripts in the British Museum* by Walter de Gray Birch, published in six volumes between 1887 and 1900. The largest catalogue of seals yet published in Britain, it contains over 23,000 entries, of which nearly 15,000 are English or Welsh, and over 2500 Scottish, but despite its size it

46 L.C. Loyd and D.M. Stenton (eds), *Sir Christopher Hatton's Book of Seals* (Oxford, 1950), pp.xxii–xxx.

47 W. Dugdale, *The Antiquities of Warwickshire* (London, 1656), pp.672–3.

48 C. Hardwick (ed.), *Historia monasterii S. Augustini Cantuariensis, by Thomas of Elmham* (Rolls Series; 1858), pp.118–19.

49 B.L. Stowe MSS. 665, 666.

omits the non-armorial personal seals which probably make up four-fifths of all British seals surviving from the middle ages. This same limitation appears in the comprehensive three-volume work by J.H. Stevenson and M. Wood, *Scottish Heraldic Seals* (1940), which includes all royal, ecclesiastical and corporate seals, whether heraldic or not, and in monographs: *English Seals* by J. Harvey Bloom (1906), Birch's two-volume *History of Scottish Seals* (1905–7) and his more general work *Seals* (1907). None pays much attention to lesser personal seals, and though John Selden in the seventeenth century had pointed out, correctly, that 'the use of Seals were promiscuous in England to persons of all qualities that would use them',[50] Bloom moves no further down the social scale than 'Seals of Private Gentlemen and of Merchants'.

It is extraordinary that interest in seals, though widespread and of long standing, was to this point almost entirely antiquarian and descriptive: their value as evidence in wider problems of social and economic history, the history of art, law and diplomatic, had been scarcely noticed and there had been little systematic work on their design, function or use. In the 1920s and 1930s, however, important research by, particularly, T.F. Tout, Hilary Jenkinson and R. Hannay threw new light on the various royal seals of medieval England and Scotland, work that has been continued by P. Chaplais and A.A.M. Duncan. This lead has only recently been followed by work on other kinds of seal, though in 1954 Jenkinson (anonymously; but it is based on a signed article of 1937) published the *Guide to Seals in the Public Record Office* that remains the best overall guide to seals in English. In the past twenty years T.A. Heslop, Brigitte Bedos-Rezak and others have begun to ask and answer basically important questions about seals, looking at them in new, wider, contexts and opening the way to new fields of research. Crucial to further investigation is knowing exactly what seals there are, and Jenkinson urged the need for catalogues of all seals, not just those of the upper classes.[51] This need has started to be met in several major repositories, most recently by the first volume of the *Catalogue of Seals in the National Museum of Wales* (1993) by D.H. Williams. At the Public Record Office R.H. Ellis produced the first three volumes of a *Catalogue of Seals*, two of personal seals (1978–81) and one of monastic (1986), to be continued in the same form for all but personal seals, which have started to be catalogued on computer, offering entirely new opportunities for comparison and analysis. The chapters that follow look at the development, design and use of the various kinds of medieval seal as understood at present; it is all too clear that there are many gaps in our knowledge, many questions that can be answered, and the picture is likely to change in the years to come.

[50] J. Selden, *Titles of Honour* (3rd edn, London, 1672), p.651 (citing the chronicle attributed to Ingulf).

[51] *Guide to Seals in the Public Record Office* (London, 1954), pp.vii–x, 1–2.

2 ROYAL SEALS

GREAT SEALS

The seal of Edward the Confessor (1042–66) is the earliest known of an English king, and on each side it shows him enthroned, in front holding a sceptre and orb and on the back a different sceptre and sword.[1] No seal is known of his successor, Harold II, but the seal of William I (1066–87) has the king on horseback in front, with legend referring to him as ruler of Normandy, and enthroned on the back, holding a sword and orb and with legend referring to the king of England. William II (1087–1100) had a seal with the same designs, but it was used the other way round, so that the equestrian side was at the back, and on both sides he is named 'rex Anglorum'. From Scotland we have no royal seal earlier than the unique impression of what is probably the seal of Duncan II, who reigned for six months in 1093–4;[2] it is single-sided, with the king on horseback. Of Edgar (1097–1107) there are impressions of what is probably just one seal, single-sided and showing the king enthroned with sword and sceptre; but the seal of Alexander I (1107–24) is two-sided and, modelled on William II's,[3] shows him enthroned with sword and orb in front and mounted on the back. From Wales, the only two-sided seal known of a native ruler belonged to David ap Llywelyn of Gwynedd (1240–6) and was possibly supplied from England by Henry III: he is enthroned in front, mounted on the back.[4] Cadell ap Gruffudd of Deheubarth (died 1175),[5] Gwenwynwyn of southern Powis (1195–1208) and Llywelyn ap Iorwerth of Gwynedd (1195–1240) all had single-sided equestrian seals.

Fig 4

Fig 23

Fig 5

Fig 24

From the time of William II in England, Alexander I in Scotland, the principal royal seal, the great seal, of almost every reign has shown the sovereign enthroned in front, and on the back mounted on a horse – a tradition that continued down to the union of the kingdoms in 1707 and on to the present day. To this design attached something of the aura of kingship

1 B. Bedos-Rezak, 'The King Enthroned, a New Theme in Anglo-Saxon Royal Iconography', in J.T. Rosenthal (ed.), *Kings and Kingship* (Binghamton, 1986), pp.62–6, discusses the details of the design and its significance. This section on the great seals draws throughout on A.B. Wyon and A. Wyon, *The Great Seals of England* (London, 1887), and on the subsequent books and articles that have corrected it, listed below in the Select Bibliography.

2 The date is discussed by W.E. Kapelle, *The Norman Conquest of the North* (London, 1979), pp.274–5.

3 As shown in an unpublished paper by Professor A.A.M. Duncan.

4 D. Crouch, *The Image of Aristocracy in Britain, 1000–1300* (London, 1992), p.246.

5 D. Crouch, 'The Earliest Original Charter of a Welsh King', *Bulletin of the Board of Celtic Studies*, 26 (1989), pp.130–1.

– it displayed the two principal facets of sovereignty, the king sitting to dispense justice and riding to lead in battle. It is interesting that when Alexander III's death left Scotland from 1286 to 1292 in the hands of guardians of the realm, they modestly used a seal that had the royal arms in front and St Andrew on the back, whereas Robert and Murdoch, dukes of Albany, the two successive governors of the kingdom from 1406 to 1424 when James

23 William I, 1066–87
The earliest known equestrian seal, showing the Conqueror on horseback in front (the legend refers to him as ruler of Normandy), enthroned on the back (the legend refers to him as king of England). This is a cast made from the best of the five surviving impressions, on a grant of 1069 to St-Denis Abbey, Paris; since it was made the original seal has seriously deteriorated.
About 8.0 cm (reduced).
British Library, Doubleday Casts A 11, 12

I was captive in England, used a seal showing them enthroned – though without crown or sceptre – and mounted. When Edward I and Edward II ruled parts of Scotland, their seal for Scotland showed the king enthroned in front, but simply the arms of England on the back; they saw Scotland not as a separate kingdom but as a department of English government. It is a measure of the standing and authority accorded to the Black Prince, Edward III's eldest son (1330–76) – apparently alone among heirs to the throne in medieval Britain – as well as to John Warenne, earl of Surrey, in 1346, that their seals, though smaller than the king's, had the same designs. It is a measure of the power and dignity of the bishops of Durham that, starting with Thomas Hatfield (1345–81), the secular seals they used as palatinate lords showed the bishop in front mounted in armour, with sword and shield and wearing a mitre on his coroneted helmet, and on the back enthroned in full vestments. And it is a measure of the challenge offered by Owen Glyndwr, who in

Fig 33
Fig 25

rebellion against English rule from 1400 to 1415 claimed to be prince of an independent Wales, that he used a great seal of the same form as the sovereign's, showing him enthroned with sceptre on the front, and on the back riding to battle with sword and crowned helmet.[6]

What was shown on the two sides of the great seals remained unaltered – but the way they presented the enthroned and mounted kings changed from

24 Llywelyn ap Iorwerth, prince of Gwynedd, 1195–1240
This single-sided equestrian seal, with counterseal, is in the style used by contemporary barons rather than the two-sided seals of the rulers of England and Scotland. The counterseal is a gem engraved with a boar beneath a tree, with legend 'Sigillum secretum Lewlini' (secret seal of Llywelyn).
Seal about 7.0 cm, counterseal 2.5 × 3.2 cm (reduced).
British Library, Cotton Charter xxiv.17

generation to generation, displaying successive developments in artistic style, clothing and ornament, armour and heraldry. The changes were broadly the same in England and in Scotland. The king's throne was first shown with an ornamented back in 1259 in England and by 1265 in Scotland and with a canopy above it in 1340 in England, 1371 in Scotland. On the reverse, the horse first appears caparisoned in Scotland in 1249, and in England in 1272. The lions of England appear on the great seal first in 1198, and in Scotland the lion rampant is shown on the king's shield in 1214 and with the royal tressure, the two-lined border with fleurs-de-lis, in 1249. Both kingdoms first had great seals entirely in renaissance style in 1542: the third

Fig 26

6 J. Doubleday, 'Great and Privy Seals of Owen Glyndowr', *Archaeologia*, 25 (1834), pp.619–20, pl.lxxi; D.H. Williams, *Welsh History through Seals* (Cardiff, 1982), p.23 (from B.L. Harley Charter 75 C.34).

25 John Fordham, bishop of Durham, 1382
Within their see the bishops of Durham exercised many of the rights that elsewhere belonged to the Crown, levying taxes and appointing their own local officials. Their status is reflected in the seals they used for secular purposes from the mid-fourteenth century onwards: two-sided, like royal great seals, showing the bishop mounted in armour on the front and enthroned with mitre and crosier on the back.

8.0 cm (reduced).
British Library, Seals liv.81, 82

26 Alexander II, 1214–49
The great seals of the English and Scottish rulers followed the same basic pattern throughout the middle ages: the king enthroned on the front and riding to battle on the back. In detail too, the designs developed similarly in the two kingdoms. Alexander II's is the first great seal to show the Scottish lion rampant on the king's shield; the border with fleurs-de-lis – the royal tressure – first appears on the first seal of his son and successor, Alexander III.

8.9 cm (reduced).
British Library, Cotton Charter xviii.2

seal of Henry VIII and the first of Mary, Queen of Scots. Over the centuries the great seals became more elaborately detailed and more finely engraved. Their size did not remain constant and over the centuries they became larger – in England from the 8-centimetre diameter of William II's seal to over 12 centimetres in the second and third seals of Henry VIII, and in Scotland, where the size was generally smaller, from under 7 centimetres in the early twelfth century to 11 centimetres in the fifteenth. For most of his minority

27 Henry VIII, second great seal, 1535–42
The last great seal of an English king in medieval form – on its successor, the king's third great seal, the throne and other detail are in renaissance style. Here already the lettering is in roman capitals instead of the black-letter forms of earlier great seals and the reversal of each letter N may reflect the engraver's unfamiliarity with the style.
12.2 cm (reduced).
British Library, Doubleday Casts A95, 96

(1249 to about 1258) Alexander III used a small seal, 4 centimetres across, showing him enthroned, with sword across his knees, in front and with the royal arms on the back; such a seal of minority is unique, and until 1252 a normal great seal was in use as well.[7]

But in any case a king did not necessarily use the same great seal throughout his reign. Sometimes we do not know the reason for the change, but often it is clear why a new seal was made. When Edward III in 1340 formally claimed to be king of France as well as of England he had a new great seal with his new title; when he renounced it at the treaty of Bretigny in 1360 a new great seal was again engraved. When the English kings went abroad

[7] G.G. Simpson, 'Kingship in Miniature: a Seal of Minority of Alexander III, 1249–1257', in A. Grant and K.J. Stringer (eds), *Medieval Scotland: Crown, Lordship and Community: Essays presented to G.W.S. Barrow* (Edinburgh, 1993), pp.131–9.

they needed a second great seal so that they could take one with them without disrupting the business of the chancery; a duplicate was provided for Henry III by 1262 and the practice continued in later reigns – sometimes the substitute seal went abroad with the king, sometimes it served as a seal of absence at home.[8] Conversely, in the fourteenth and fifteenth centuries, in both Scotland and England, a single matrix, suitably altered, might serve for the great seal of a succession of kings – perhaps for economy, but perhaps also to underline continuity of rule. Thus, Edward I's great seal was used by Edward II with a castle engraved on each side of the throne, and by Edward

28 Henry IV and Henry V, gold seal, 1408–20
The matrix of this so-called gold seal was probably of silver gilt. It is one of the most elaborate and finely engraved of the medieval great seals; the figures around the enthroned king on the front include St Michael and St George – each killing a dragon – King Edward the Confessor and King Edmund the Martyr. After the Treaty of Troyes in 1420 the legend was altered to call the king heir to the realm of France, and the seal continued in occasional use until 1460.
12.4 cm (reduced).
British Library, Additional Charter 11158

III, in the first year of his reign, with a fleur-de-lis added above each castle. In Scotland the great seal first engraved in 1406 for Robert, duke of Albany, as governor of the kingdom, continued in use until the death of James V in 1542, with altered legends and with successive changes in the design. In the reigns of Henry IV, Henry V and Henry VI the seal made for Edward III in 1360 was still being used with its legend altered – but a new golden (or silver-gilt) seal was made in about 1408, and which of the two seals was regularly used seems to have varied from time to time. *Fig 28*

[8] P. Chaplais, *Piers Gaveston: Edward II's Adoptive Brother* (Oxford, 1994), pp.38–41.

In England by the end of the thirteenth century routine legal writs and other less important documents were normally sealed with an impression not of the whole great seal but of the top half only of its two sides. This was called – confusingly – the foot of the seal, *pes sigilli*, or, by the sixteenth century, the half seal. In the seventeenth century, and perhaps much earlier, the seal might be impressed on an even smaller piece of wax, to show just the sovereign's head on each side.[9] In Scotland too, impressions of the top half only of the great seal are known from the 1370s onwards, and special mat-

29 Forged seal of Edward the Confessor, mid-twelfth century
Long thought to be a genuine seal of the Confessor, it is now known that the matrix was made a hundred years later, probably at Westminster Abbey, to seal fabricated royal grants; only the back is reproduced here. Comparison with the king's genuine seal (fig.4) shows that its design was closely copied. Other seals – of the Confessor, William I and William II – were also forged at Westminster or other Benedictine abbeys. The intention was not outright fraud, but confirmation of rights genuinely held or claimed.
7.0 cm (actual size).
British Library, Seals xxxiv.3

rices were used, possibly already in the 1440s and certainly under James V at the beginning of the sixteenth century, in the shape of a semi-circle with the two corners truncated; this was called the quarter seal.

A man who forged Henry II's seal was saved from being hanged only through the king's mercy, and by the thirteenth century in England counterfeiting the king's seal was a recognised felony, to be punished by death and forfeiture of property.[10] However, two groups of documents with forged royal seals have succeeded in deceiving later generations. The first group dates from the twelfth century. At Durham, letters were written in favour of the cathedral priory, and a forged seal of Henry I attached, early in his own reign. In the 1150s documents were forged at Westminster Abbey and perhaps elsewhere in favour of five Benedictine abbeys – Battle, Coventry, Gloucester, Ramsey and Westminster itself – with false seals of Edward the

9 H.C. Maxwell-Lyte, *Historical Notes on the Use of the Great Seal of England* (London, 1926), pp.304–9.

10 M.R. James, C.N.L. Brooke and R.A.B. Mynors (eds), *Walter Map De nugis curialium: Courtiers' Trifles* (Oxford, 1983), p.495; G.E. Woodbine and S.E. Thorne (eds), *Bracton De legibus et consuetudinibus Angliae* (Cambridge, Mass., 4v., 1968–77), ii, p.337; iii, p.307.

Confessor, William I and William II. All these forgeries were made from specially engraved matrices – and a contemporary lead matrix still exists for forging a seal of Henry II. The documents were probably written in support of rights genuinely believed to exist, and it was shown only in 1957 and 1960 that Edward the Confessor had one great seal not three, William I and William II one each not two and Henry I three not four, as had been supposed.[11] The second group of forgeries was unmasked in 1837, though there had been earlier doubts. John Hardyng, employed by Henry V to gather evidence in Scotland for English claims to overlordship, delivered relevant documents to the king in 1422 and others later to Henry VI and Edward IV, winning royal favour and rewards. Most of these documents that can be identified are forgeries, and with them are specially created seals of Robert III, David II and – most remarkably – Malcolm III (1057–93), whose seal bears wholly anachronistic royal arms.[12]

Fig 29

Royal seal matrices might be destroyed ceremonially. When Edward III, after some months on the throne, finally replaced the great seal that his father and grandfather had used, it was broken into tiny pieces in his presence.[13] Sometimes there were political considerations. In 1292 the seal of the guardians of the Scottish kingdom was broken up in recognition of Edward I's overlordship, and earlier, in 1284, the seals of the defeated princes of Gwynedd, Llywelyn ap Gruffudd and his brother David, and of Llywelyn's wife Eleanor, had been made into a chalice.[14] It was not just security but the symbolism attaching to the seal that was at issue.

PRIVY SEALS, SECRET SEALS, SIGNETS

As far as we know, William I had only one seal. Henry VII, more than four hundred years later, in 1509, attested his will with his sign manual and with his great seal, his privy seal, the signet that was kept by the secretary and the privy signet with the eagle, which he kept himself.[15] Behind this change lies the whole development of the medieval English royal chancery, in origin the writing office in the king's household and thus the natural home of the seal that authenticated what was written and sent out. In broad outline the course of this development is straightforward. The amount and nature of its business made it increasingly impracticable for this writing office to continue within the king's household, which still in the early fourteenth century was

[11] P. Chaplais, 'The Seals and Original Charters of Henry I', *English Historical Review*, 75 (1960), pp.260–75; T.A.M. Bishop and P. Chaplais (eds), *Facsimiles of English Royal Writs to A.D.1100* (Oxford, 1957), pp.xix–xxiv; A.B. Tonnochy, *Catalogue of British Seal-Dies in the British Museum* (London, 1952), p.4.

[12] F. Palgrave (ed.), *Documents and Records Illustrating the History of Scotland* (Record Commission; 1837), pp.cxcvi–ccxxiv; cf. T. Astle, 'An Account of the Seals of the Kings, Royal Boroughs, and Magnates of Scotland', *Vetusta Monumenta*, vol.iii (Society of Antiquaries; 1796), pp.6–8.

[13] *Calendar of Close Rolls 1327–30*, p.227.

[14] E.L.G Stones and G.G. Simpson (eds), *Edward I and the Throne of Scotland* (Oxford, 2v., 1978), ii, pp.252–3; A.J. Taylor, 'A Fragment of a *Dona* Account of 1284', *Bulletin of the Board of Celtic Studies*, 27 (1976–8), pp.256–8.

[15] T. Astle (ed.), *The Will of King Henry the Seventh* (London, 1775), pp.46–7.

constantly on the move; chancery, and with it the great seal in the chancellor's care, acquired a permanent home, away from the court. This process had begun in the mid-thirteenth century and by 1310 at latest chancery was fully established at Westminster. But the king still needed a writing office in his household and a seal to authenticate its documents; this was the privy seal, which in turn in the early fourteenth century acquired a special keeper and a fixed establishment, and while not fully divorced from the royal household it passed from the king's immediate control, leaving him with his secre-

30 Signet ring of Richard I, 1189–99
The impression on the right is from this simple signet ring believed to be Richard I's – the legend reads 'S' Richard re[g?] p' (private seal of King Richard). The gem is plasma and it was probably engraved in the fifth century with the figure of Mercury; the ring and setting are gold. The legend has been defaced with a series of punched lines, perhaps to invalidate it after the king's death.
1.7 × 1.4 cm (enlarged).
British Museum, Department of Medieval and Later Antiquities, 1962–11–1 1

tary and an official signet. But apart from these formal, official seals, the king must have needed one or more seals that he always carried, or wore in a ring, to authenticate immediate orders. We know that Richard I had such a private seal, whether or not the signet ring attributed to him was really his;[16] his predecessors may well have had similar seals, even in the eleventh century. Likewise in 1220 and 1230 Llywelyn ap Iorwerth, ruler of Gwynedd, sent letters under his privy or secret seal, and when his grandson Llywelyn ap Gruffudd was killed in battle in 1282 his small seal was found on his person.[17]

Fig 24

A great deal of very detailed work has been done on the household administration of the medieval English kings and on the successive development of the chancery, the privy seal office and the signet office. In Scotland similar processes were at work, though they have not been so exhaustively studied –

16 P. Chaplais, *English Royal Documents, King John – Henry VI* (Oxford, 1971), p.24.

17 J.G. Edwards (ed.), *Calendar of Correspondence concerning Wales* (Board of Celtic Studies, History and Law Series, 2; 1935), pp.24, 51, 129.

indeed, the records that would make this possible do not exist. But in both countries two difficulties arise when we look at the seals themselves alongside the administrative structures that made use of them. One is that the terminology of the records is sometimes less exact than we might wish, and there is a recurrent problem over the word *secretum*, which at different periods and in different contexts was applied to any royal seal except the great seal. The other difficulty is that whereas the great seal was for outward communication – practically every impression that was made passed out of

31 Signet of Henry V, 1413–22
This was the official seal directly under the control of the king of England and the secretary in the royal household – by the fifteenth century it was quite distinct from the personal seal that the king carried or wore in a ring.
3.2 cm (enlarged).
British Library, Doubleday Cast A 85

the hands of the government central offices – these other seals were mostly used within the administration itself. This means not necessarily that they were less likely to survive, but that they were less widespread, less well known to contemporaries and generally less familiar to antiquaries and historians.

The formally constituted privy seal of the English kings was always single-sided, with legend beginning 'Secretum . . .' (except one privy seal of Edward III) and with the royal arms as its design – whence documents in French called it *la targe*, the shield. There are references to the *sigillum parvum* or *privatum sigillum* of Richard I and John, and Henry III had a privy seal with the royal arms on it, but the first known from an existing impression is Edward I's. Like the great seal, the privy seal got larger in the course of time: Edward I's was 2.5 centimetres across, Henry VII's 6 centimetres. In the fifteenth century, when its use was formalised, the signet also bore the royal arms. But the king's small personal seals, from which both privy seal and signet took their origins, were more varied – and the less formal the seal, the less we should look for continuity of design or for systematic sequence of use. The signet attributed to Richard I has a gem with a standing figure, probably Minerva, and a legend which, with abbreviations extended, is read as 'Sigillum Richard regis privatum'. John before his accession used as a counterseal a gem with a woman's head inscribed 'Sigillum secretum' and this may well have been the privy seal that he used as king. Small equestrian seals were used by Edward II (with legend beginning 'Sigillum secretum . . .') and Edward III ('Signetum . . .'), and Edward II also had a seal with a griffin on it, his *secretum sigillum vocatum Griffoun* (private seal called griffin).

Fig 30

There was duplication of these personal seals, along with the growing formalisation of the signet. One seal of Richard II had a shield combining the royal arms with the supposed arms of Edward the Confessor, and the seal of the eagle which Henry VII used on his will first appears in 1421 – a small oval with a double-headed eagle and Latin quotation from the Bible, 'as the eagle inciting its young to fly' (Deuteronomy 32.11).[18]

32 Privy seal of James II, 1437–60
The kings of Scotland were regularly using privy seals from the early fourteenth century. This seal, engraved for James II, was used by his three successors down to 1542, but tiny alterations were made to the design on the accession of James III and James IV.
6.0 cm (actual size).
British Library, Seal xlvii.68

In Scotland Alexander III (1249–86) and John Balliol (1292–6) probably both had privy seals but no impression is known and the earliest surviving privy seals are of Robert I (1306–29) – single-sided, with the royal arms and with the word 'secretum' in the legend. The demands of a dispersed administration may have meant that the four or five privy seals of Robert I were used concurrently.[19] As in England the privy seals increased in size: one of Robert I's was only 2.7 centimetres across, while the single privy seal which, with minor alterations, served James II and his three successors from 1437 to 1542, was 6 centimetres. David II in 1359 used a signet inscribed 'Secretum regis Scocie', an oval gem with a crouching lion and the letters MB, which suggest that it may have belonged to his grandmother, Marjory Bruce, and thus also to his father, Robert I. There are late-fourteenth-century references to the king's signet and signet ring, but no impressions are known. From James I to James V every king had one or more signets with the lion rampant and royal tressure and, mysteriously, the word 'Marchmond', the alternative name for Roxburgh, evidence perhaps of the importance attached to retaking this border fortress. James II, James III and James IV also had what may have been a more personal signet with a unicorn. By the late fifteenth century

Fig 32

18 Maxwell-Lyte, *Historical Notes*, pp.41–7, 101–7, 109–10, 112–17; Chaplais, *English Royal Documents*, pp.23–6, 34–5; P.E. Lasko, 'The Signet Ring of King Richard I of England', *Journal of the Society of Archivists*, 1, no.8 (1963), p.333–5; W.S. Walford and A. Way, 'Examples of Mediaeval Seals', *Archaeological Journal*, 18 (1861), pp.49–55.

19 A.A.M. Duncan (ed.), *The Acts of Robert I, King of Scots 1306–1329* (Regesta Regum Scottorum, vol.5; Edinburgh, 1988), pp.186–8.

the lion signets were in formal use and in 1524 there were three signets – the great signet and one other held by the secretary, and one held by the king.[20]

DEPUTED GREAT SEALS

One sort of royal seal that was used in England but not in medieval Scotland was the deputed or departmental great seal. The description of the exchequer, *Dialogus de scaccario*, that was written by Richard FitzNigel in the late 1170s, tells how it used a seal of the king that was kept by the treasurer in a purse sealed by the chancellor and brought out by the chancellor's authority when the exchequer met; this seal had the same design and legend as the great seal, 'the itinerant seal of the king's court', so that 'the two seals may be recognised as of equal authority in commanding'.[21] This was the first of the departmental seals, which counted in all respects as great seals, carrying the same royal authority, but which were for use in business conducted in the king's name away from both the royal household and the chancery.

The *Dialogus de scaccario* shows that Henry II's exchequer seal was an exact duplicate of his great seal, but all departmental seals that we know from surviving impressions have on the front the king either enthroned or mounted, and on the back the royal arms. The earliest we have are from the exchequer, which used equestrian seals; they date from the reign of Edward I, but it has been thought from their style that the matrices were a little older. The courts of common pleas and king's bench each first acquired its own seal, showing the king enthroned, probably in 1344; in 1338 there had been complaints that they were sending out writs under the seals of the justices themselves instead of under the great seal or the seal of the exchequer. In both courts and in the exchequer a single seal might be made to last over many reigns – in the common pleas apparently from 1344 to the time of Henry VIII, some two hundred years – but with so many successive alterations of legend and design that a process of casting may have been used to introduce new flat surfaces instead of simply re-engraving the matrices.[22]

Similar deputed great seals were used by the chamberlains who were in charge of the royal administration of North Wales and of South Wales. Few impressions survive, and none before the fifteenth century, but they presumably originated in 1284, when Edward I set up this structure of government. The North Wales impressions are probably later than those we have from South Wales; the seal is certainly later in style, and instead of the royal arms it has the arms of North Wales on the reverse. In this it parallels the contemporary royal seals for the palatinates of Chester and Lancaster, which can also be viewed as deputed great seals – at Chester the royal arms on the

[20] R.K. Hannay, 'The Early History of the Scottish Signet', in *The Society of Writers to His Majesty's Signet* (Edinburgh, 1936), pp.6–32; W.C. Dickinson, ' "Our Signet of the Unicorn" ', *Scottish Historical Review*, 26 (1947), p.147–8.

[21] C. Johnson (ed.), *The Course of the Exchequer by Richard, Son of Nigel* (London, 1950), pp.19, 62.

[22] H. Jenkinson, 'The Great Seal of England: Deputed or Departmental Seals', *Archaeologia*, 85 (1936), pp.296–303; B. Wilkinson, 'The Seals of the Two Benches under Edward III', *English Historical Review*, 42 (1927), pp.397–401.

33 Seal of Edward I for the government of Scotland, 1296–1307
In front is the king enthroned, as on the great seal, but on the back is not the king on horseback but simply the royal arms. This is the same pattern as the duplicate great seals – deputed seals – used in departments of government in England and Wales.
8.6 cm (reduced).
British Library, Seals xlvii.23, 24

reverse were combined with the arms of Edward the Confessor on Richard II's seal (just as they were on the king's signet) but with the arms of Chester itself in the fifteenth century.[23] It is interesting how neatly the seal for Scotland of Edward I and Edward II fits into this pattern: with the king enthroned on the front, royal arms on the back, it was simply a deputed great seal of England.

Fig 33

SEALS OF OFFICIALS

The deputed great seals implied the full authority, indeed the notional presence, of the king in person. But in both England and Scotland there were royal officers in the central organs of government as well as in its local administration who, as agents of the king's business, had their own official seals. Among them only the English seals for recognisances, acknowledgments of debt – which will be discussed along with town seals – have ever been systematically studied. In fact, these seals of officials could probably tell us a good deal of the workings of royal administration, especially locally, of its development over the years, and of the concepts underlying it. There are certainly questions about them that research might answer: when did seals for particular offices originate? how far were the matrices supplied centrally? how rigidly were their designs controlled? what distinctions were main-

[23] Jenkinson, 'The Great Seal of England: Deputed or Departmental Seals', pp.325–7, 332–5.

34 Richard, duke of Gloucester, as admiral for Dorset and Somerset, 1461–2
The admirals of fifteenth-century England used seals with a ship bearing either the royal arms or their own arms on the sail. Here the arms are of Richard himself, the same as his brother, the king, but distinguished with an heraldic label at the top. At the front of the ship are an anchor and, above, a cresset or fire-basket.
7.6 cm (actual size).
British Library, Doubleday Cast G 269

tained between personal and official seals? – and many more. Here we can look at only a few of these seals and at some of the questions they raise.

One question is, who in fact had official seals? The greatest officers of state did not, in either Scotland or England. There were no official seals for the chancellor or treasurer, for the chief justices of the two benches in England or for the great chamberlain in Scotland – except, perhaps significantly, under Edward II before Bannockburn. Nor were these offices mentioned on their holders' personal seals. On the other hand, hereditary office might be included in personal seals' legends: the Lacy earls of Lincoln were there named as constables of Chester, the earls of Lancaster as stewards of England, and in Scotland the Stewart family, whose office as royal steward gave them their name, were *dapifer regis*, *seneschallus regis Scocie* on their seals from the twelfth century onwards. And certain lesser high offices consistently had official seals, at least in the later middle ages. From fifteenth-century England we have a series of seals of lord high admirals and of the admirals for particular parts of the coast; all have the same design, a ship sailing to the left with the arms of the king or of the admiral himself on the sail, and the admiral is named in the legend. Henry Percy, earl of Northumberland (1455–61), had a special seal as warden of the East March. From Scotland there are seals for the justiciars north of the Forth and south of the Forth, with either the king's initial and crown or the royal arms; the earliest impression known dates from 1366, and they are all seals of the office itself, naming the office but not the holder in the legend.

Fig 34

Seals of English sheriffs are known from the early fourteenth century onwards.[24] Nearly all include a triple-towered castle in their design, along

[24] C.H. Hunter Blair, 'The Sheriffs of Northumberland', *Archaeologia Aeliana*, 4th ser. 20 (1942), pp.20–1; J. Cherry, 'Imago Castelli: the Depiction of Castles on Medieval Seals', *Château Gaillard: Études de castellologie médiévale*, 15 (1992), pp.86–7.

with the sheriff's initials, coat of arms or crest, but they are so varied that they were almost certainly procured by the sheriffs themselves. The Statute of Cambridge in 1388 ordered that labourers moving from the area where they lived should be given a pass sealed by someone appointed by the local justices of the peace, and described the seal's design – it should name the county around the edge and the hundred, wapentake or town across the

35 Seal for labourers' passes, late fourteenth century
Passes for labourers moving from one area to another were sealed by order of justices of the peace, and the design of the seal was laid down by a statute of 1388. Around the edge it was to name the county – here 'S' Com' Cantebrygg', Cambridgeshire – and across the centre the hundred, wapentake or town – here 'Stapylho', Staploe Hundred.
2.8 cm (enlarged).
British Library, Seal lx.59

Fig 35 centre.[25] Three years later sheriffs were ordered to have these seals made at once, and at least six of the matrices survive, showing minor variations within the definition of the statute.[26] We would expect similar variations in the seals for local collectors of the successive taxes on movables though too few are recorded to show this. On the other hand the two-sided seals for the customs service were provided centrally; what are probably the earliest, issued when the duty and the permanent officers to collect it were instituted in 1275, have the lions of England on both sides – in front on a shield – with legends naming the port in front and 'Pro lanis et coreis liberandis' on the

36 Cocket seal for Inverness and Cromarty, fifteenth century
The cocket seal was used by local officials collecting customs duties for the Crown. Some, like this, bore the royal arms; others had the figure of a saint. This is a modern impression from a matrix that was found on the seashore near Aberdeen in about 1812.
5.4 cm (actual size).
British Library, Seal xlvii.823

25 *Statutes of the Realm* (Record Commission; 11v., 1810–28), ii, p.56.
26 *Calendar of Close Rolls 1389–92*, pp.255–6; Tonnochy, *Catalogue of Seal-Dies*, pp.27–32.

Fig 36 back. On the other hand, the analogous Scottish cocket offices – for collecting duties and certifying their payment – used seals of varied types. Unless or until many more local official seals come to light from both countries we cannot hope to discover how most were designed, supplied or used.

3 ARISTOCRATIC AND HERALDIC SEALS

MOUNTED KNIGHTS AND STANDING LADIES

The ownership and use of seals was not restricted to royalty. By the end of the eleventh century some of the Anglo-Norman aristocracy were already using seals, a practice that spread rapidly in the first half of the twelfth century. Their Norman forebears before the Conquest may or may not have used seals. Certainly until the late twelfth century the almost universal design of upper-class men's seals was a mounted knight, a design that stemmed directly from the seal of William I. Like the king's great seal, these equestrian seals were a personification of their owners, a powerful image of their social standing and military skills. Alternative designs were few. A remarkably lifelike lion appears on a seal of William, earl of Gloucester, that had probably belonged to his father, Robert (died 1147); Robert was an illegitimate son of Henry I, and Henry had used a lion as his emblem.[1] Baldwin de Redvers, first earl of Devon (1141–55), and possibly his four successors down to 1217, had seals showing a griffin attacking an elephant; the subject was drawn from the bestiary, but why it was chosen we do not know.[2] But these were exceptional. The pattern was set in England by the 1090s, when Stephen, count of Aumâle, and Ilbert de Lacy were among those already using equestrian seals;[3] their spread from the top of society throughout its upper reaches has never been charted, but by the accession of Henry II in 1154 probably any knight might have one. The future David I of Scotland was using an equestrian seal in about 1120, but few private charters are known from Scotland before the mid-twelfth century and these seals may not have become widespread there until the 1160s; the earliest Welsh examples date from perhaps the 1140s.[4] In both Scotland and Wales, however, their apparently late adoption may point simply to the loss of sealed documents from the early twelfth century.

Fig 37

The equestrian seals of the twelfth and thirteenth centuries were large, typically from 4.5 to 8 centimetres across – generally speaking, the more important magnates had the largest seals. They were circular, with few exceptions – William de Londres in the mid-twelfth century had one that was

1 R.B. Patterson (ed.), *Earldom of Gloucester Charters* (Oxford, 1973), p.24, pl.XXXI.

2 R. Bearman (ed.), *Charters of the Redvers Family and the Earldom of Devon, 1090–1217* (Devon and Cornwall Record Society, new ser. 37; 1994), pp.50–1.

3 D. Crouch, *The Image of Aristocracy in Britain, 1000–1300* (London, 1992), p.187; M.T. Clanchy, *From Memory to Written Record* (2nd edn, Oxford, 1993), pl.I.

4 M.P. Siddons, 'Welsh Equestrian Seals', *National Library of Wales Journal*, 23 (1983–4), pp.309–11.

37 Earl David, c.1120
One of the earliest Scottish equestrian seals, owned by the future David I. As often before the 1180s, the horse is standing or walking, not galloping, and the kite-shaped shield is held away from view on the rider's left. However, the banner – or gonfanon – might bear a pre-heraldic design, here a rose-shaped device.

7.0 cm (actual size).
Dean and Chapter of Durham, Miscellaneous Charter 759

38 Roger de Quincy, earl of Winchester, c.1235
An unusual two-sided seal copied from one of Roger's father, Saher de Quincy. Here Roger is named as earl of Winchester in front, constable of Scotland on the back, but his father did not have the latter title and on his seal the legend places the combat with the lion in a biblical context, with possible political overtones – Saher was a leader of the barons against King John. There are no further examples of this design, but a few other equestrian seals have a dragon or wyvern below the horse.

7.4 cm (reduced).
Public Record Office, DL 27/203

an horizontal oval, Richard de Clare, earl of Hertford (1173–1217), an octagonal one and Morgan Gam (died 1241) a pointed oval.[5] At first they were nearly all single-sided, but an English magnate with two titles might have a two-sided seal with a mounted knight on each side, naming him with one title on the front, the other on the back. Examples are the seals of Alan, his son Conan and grandson-in-law Geoffrey, count and dukes of Brittany and earls of Richmond (1136–86), and another is the seal of Gilbert de Clare, earl of Gloucester and Hertford (1262–95). Exceptional is the two-sided seal of *Fig 38* Roger de Quincy in about 1235 – one side as earl of Winchester, the other as hereditary constable of Scotland – which has him mounted in front, and on the back fighting a lion on foot. The horse nearly always faces the right, as on royal great seals, but exceptions include seals of Saher de Quincy, earl of Winchester (1207–19), Morgan Gam and Patrick, earl of Dunbar (1248–89). The rider carries a shield in the left hand, and a sword brandished in the right. Occasionally, however, the sword is replaced by an equally potent symbol, the lance with a pennon, as on seals of the future David I of Scotland and Saher de Quincy, and this is how the king is shown on the first great seals of both Scotland and England. Curiously, although in Scotland a sword replaced the lance on the great seal only in 1214, some sixty years later than the lance's final disappearance from the great seal in England, Scottish equestrian seals with a lance seem even rarer than English ones.

The design otherwise scarcely varies, though in the thirteenth century other elements were occasionally introduced. There are trees or bushes below the rider on the seals of Alexander Stewart (about 1226) and Humphrey de Bohun, earl of Hertford and Essex (1236–75), a threatening dragon

39 Robert FitzWalter, c.1207–15
This silver seal-matrix is of the finest workmanship. The shield held in front of the rider bears the arms of the FitzWalters (chevrons) and in front of the horse is another shield with the arms of their cousins and close political allies, the Quincy family (voided lozenges). Below the horse is a wyvern, a two-legged dragon.

7.2 cm (actual size).
British Museum, Department of Medieval and Later Antiquities, Seal-Die no.332

[5] Siddons, 'Welsh Equestrian Seals', pp.299, 309, 314, 318; B.L. Additional Charter 47953 (cited by Crouch, *Image of Aristocracy*, p.242n).

40 Seal and counterseal of Simon de Montfort, earl of Leicester, c.1239
An equestrian seal in hunting style, showing the rider blowing a horn and with a hound running below, a tree behind. On the counterseal are the Montfort arms, a lion rampant with forked tail – in the thirteenth century armorial counterseals often replaced the gems that had been usual earlier. The counterseal, the magnate's personal seal, confirmed the authentication of the seal, but might also be used separately on less important documents.

Seal 7.3 cm, counterseal 3.2 cm (reduced).
British Library, Additional Charter 11296

(with four legs) or wyvern (with two) on those of Robert FitzWalter (early thirteenth century), Roger de Quincy, earl of Winchester (1235–64), and Malise, earl of Strathearn (1271–1313). More radically, a few seals abandoned the military image altogether; instead, the rider is shown hunting, blowing a horn and with a hound beside the horse. One example of about 1170 belonged to Robert son of *Fubertus* (Fulbert or Hubert), of Stenton in East Lothian. Others, better known, are the seals of Simon de Montfort, father and son, earls of Leicester (c.1205–1265). We can find continental parallels to the equestrian huntsman's seal; it is easy enough to link them with the Montfort family, much harder to see their connection with the seal of a mid-twelfth century knight of the Scottish Lowlands. Other late-twelfth-century Scottish seals, however, show the rider with neither sword nor hound, but with a hawk, engaged in falconry – the seals of William son of John of Teviotdale in Roxburghshire and of William de Lindsay, ancestor of the earls of Crawford.

Fig 39 *Fig 40*

But if the overall design of the equestrian seal was unchanging, its details were not; the seal-engravers kept horse and rider up-to-date in their equip-

41 Roger de Mowbray, c.1155
A design of fleurs-de-lis covers the rider's shield, skirts, saddlecloth and helmet. In some families a particular design was used regularly, eventually becoming their hereditary coat of arms – but the Mowbray family arms were to be a lion, and the fleurs-de-lis here are probably simple ornament.
8.3 cm (actual size).
British Library, Seal lxxx.23

ment, thus supplying valuable information to the historian.[6] A caparison on the horse is shown intermittently from the mid-twelfth century, but appears invariably only from the mid-thirteenth; surcoats can be found worn over the armour from the mid-twelfth century and became normal in the thirteenth, and early in the thirteenth century the cylindrical helmet covering the whole face replaced the dome-shaped helmet on the top of the head. Earlier, in the course of the twelfth century, the shield had become shorter and was carried in front of the rider instead of at the left side, so that, with the horse facing the right, the shield's face was now visible on the seal – an especially interesting change, as it helps us to observe the emergence of heraldry, for which seals provide the earliest and most reliable evidence. In the early twelfth century magnates began to have easily recognised designs on their banners or shields – the seal of the future David I in about 1120 has a rose-shaped device on the banner. Before long, some seals show shield, armour and saddle-cloth completely covered with an ornamental design – Waleran, count of Meulan and earl of Worcester, had a chequered pattern in about 1140, Roger de Mowbray in about 1155 had fleur-de-lis. Such designs used regularly by particular individuals or families were the origin of inherited coats of arms. The three chevrons of the Clare family can be traced back to the multiple chevrons that were appearing on their seals by the 1140s. One of the earliest heraldic devices to appear on a seal was the lion rampant on shield and caparison of William fitz Empress, younger brother of

Fig 37

Fig 41

[6] Much of what follows, particularly on the emergence and early development of heraldry on seals, draws on C.H. Hunter Blair, 'Armorials upon English Seals from the Twelfth to the Sixteenth Centuries', *Archaeologia*, 89 (1943), pp.1–26.

42 Matilda, queen of Henry I, 1100–18
The earliest known seal of a lay woman in Britain. As queen, she wears a crown and holds sceptre and orb. Matilda's seal resembles that of her sister-in-law, Cecilia, abbess of Caen, and it may have been modeled on the seal of Matilda, William I's queen – the legend calls her Matilda the Second, queen of England.
8.0 × 5.5 cm (actual size).
British Library, Seal xlv.5

Henry II, between 1156 and 1163. Another was the broad chequered band (fess checky) of the Stewart family on the seal of Alan son of Walter in about 1170. In the first half of the thirteenth century, when heraldry began to be systematised, the shields on many equestrian seals bore their owners' coats of arms.

For women in the twelfth or thirteenth century the equivalent of the man's equestrian seal was a pointed oval with a standing female figure. The earliest *Fig 42* known seal of a lay woman in Britain is of this type. It belonged to Matilda, queen of Henry I, and shows her with crown, sceptre and orb. It may have been modelled on the seal of her sister-in-law, Cecilia, abbess of Caen, or – as it calls her *Mathildis secunda* – the lost seal of Matilda, William I's queen.[7] Lesser women were shown, full or three-quarter face, usually with a lily in the right hand – a symbol of the Virgin Mary – or a hawk in the left – a sign of high social standing – or with both, as on the late-twelfth-century seal of *Fig 43* Idonea de Hurst, of Broomhill in Sussex. There were variations on this design, among them a small dog below the figure, a flowering branch on either side, or patterning over the whole field. In the thirteenth century the figure is often shown standing on a carved bracket, or even with an architectural canopy above; the hawk began to appear more often than the lily and there are a few round seals where the woman appears on horseback, *Fig 44* either with hawk, as Mabel de Gatton, or without, as Joan de Stuteville. But the most significant change was the introduction of heraldry. On men's seals it appeared all but spontaneously on the shield and trappings; on women's seals it had to be consciously introduced on shields of arms either held by the

[7] T.A. Heslop in G. Zarnecki, J. Holt and T. Holland (eds), *English Romanesque Art 1066–1200* (London, 1984), p.305.

43 Idonea de Hurst, late twelfth century
The standing female figure in a pointed oval was by now the regular seal design for a lady. Here she holds a lily symbolising the Virgin Mary and a hawk indicating her social status – one or other was often included.
7.0 × 4.5 cm (actual size).
British Library, Campbell Charter xxv.20

44 Joan de Stuteville, 1265–75
An unusual seal in many respects. Unlike the normal seal of a lady – a standing figure in a pointed oval – it is round and shows her on horseback, riding sidesaddle. Instead of a hawk she carries a shield, and though Joan had two husbands the arms on the shield are her father's, probably to emphasise her position as his sole heiress.
About 6.0 cm (actual size).
British Library, Cotton Charter xxix.63

figure or on either side of it. Joan de Stuteville carried the arms only of her father, not of either of her two husbands, but this was unusual – normally the arms of both the father and the husband would appear. The seal of Margaret de Quincy, countess of Winchester, in about 1220 is an early example: besides two shields hanging from a tree beside her, the cinquefoil of her father's arms appears above her and her dress is embroidered with the lozenge outlines (mascles) of her husband's. Later, in 1282, the seal of Devorguilla, wife of John de Balliol, had two shields of arms on each side: those of her husband, her father and two forebears.

Fig 45

It is not just that seals provide crucial evidence for the development of heraldry: the development of heraldry had a profound effect on the design of

45 Margaret de Quincy, countess of Winchester, c.1220
By the early thirteenth century, heraldry had begun to appear on noblewomen's seals. The upper shield on the left bears the voided lozenges of Margaret's husband, and on the lower shield are the chevrons of the FitzWalters, her husband's cousins and political allies – both arms appear also on Robert FitzWalter's seal (fig.39). The cinquefoil above the figure's head is from the arms of Margaret's father and the dress is also embroidered with her husband's lozenge outlines.
About 8.0 × 5.0 cm (actual size).
British Library, Harley Charter 112 C.27

seals themselves. In the course of the thirteenth century the usual seal for an upper-class layman came to have a shield of arms as its central feature, and this continued to the sixteenth century and later. This is not to say that there were no more seals with mounted knights or standing ladies – the equestrian image was still the most striking symbol of feudal power and status – but it was mostly only the upper reaches of the aristocracy who used them, and they equally used other sorts of seal as well. The successors of the lesser knights who had equestrian seals in the twelfth century, as well as many of their betters, had heraldic seals instead.

Given that they belonged especially to the richest people, it is not surprising that in the fourteenth and fifteenth centuries most of these equestrian and ladies' seals were finely engraved and tended to become more elaborate. The field behind the rider might be patterned or decorated with branches or flowers, the standing figure placed in a complex setting with carved corbel below, crocketed canopy above and traceried niches on either side. Engravers continued to keep in step with changing fashions of armour and horse-trappings, dress and architecture – thus, at the end of the thirteenth century helmets acquired crests and the caparisons, formerly stiff, became soft and flowing. Many of the seals were two-sided, with a heraldic design on the back – indeed, this was already happening in the thirteenth century. A very few equestrian seals, as we have seen, had an enthroned figure on the other side: John Warenne, the Black Prince, the bishops of Durham. Sometimes quite a small seal would use one or other of the two old aristocratic designs, and there are Scottish examples, from the top of the social scale, of a standing lady, with shields, on a small circular seal: one belonged to Margaret Stewart, countess of Angus and Mar in 1378, another to Margaret Leslie, lady of the Isles and countess of Ross in 1420. Mostly, however, these seals were large, which reflected their owners' status but was not without

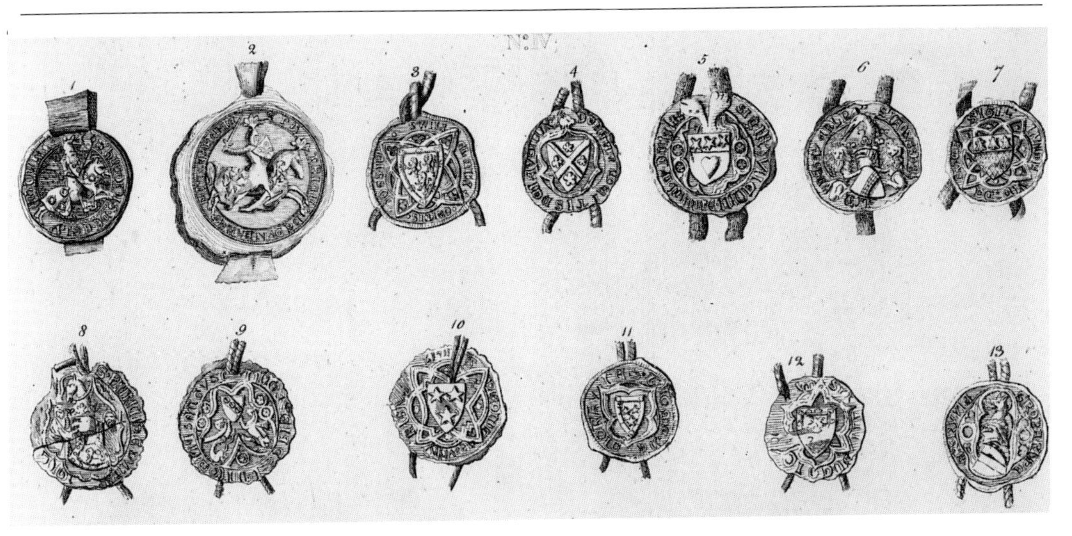

46 Equestrian and heraldic seals from Scotland, fourteenth and fifteenth centuries
Part of a plate from 'An Account of the Seals of the Kings, Royal Boroughs and Magnates of Scotland' by Thomas Astle, published in 1796 by the Society of Antiquaries of London in *Vetusta Monumenta*, vol.3. It shows a typical range of late-medieval heraldic seals. Included are both equestrian (no.2) and armorial (no.8) seals of Patrick de Dunbar, earl of March 1308–68.
British Library, 748.h.5

risk: it was held to be a sign of the treasonable intentions of Thomas, earl of Lancaster, that he owned a seal larger than Edward II's[8] – as indeed it was, by about a centimetre, equestrian in front, heraldic at the back. For the upper classes the seal was a personification, the public image, of its owner – and this appears no less clearly in the heraldic seals.

HERALDIC SEALS

Seals have for centuries been used as a source of evidence for the arms of particular persons and families and for the development of heraldry in general. It is surprising, then, that so little work has been done on the development of the heraldic seal itself, of its various forms and successive changes in style. An exact chronology, national or regional, could be constructed without great difficulty, as we have further information about most of the people who used heraldic seals, and from the late thirteenth century the deeds to which most are attached all give the precise date in their text.

Precursors of the heraldic seal were used about 1150–60 by Rohese de Gant, wife of the earl of Lincoln and daughter of Richard FitzGilbert of Clare, and by her daughter Alice – each was a pointed oval, with the field

[8] C.H. Hunter Blair, 'A Note upon Mediaeval Seals with Special Reference to those in Durham Treasury', *Archaeologia Aeliana*, 3rd ser. 17 (1920), p.260, citing no source.

47 Seal and counterseal of Roger de Lacy, c.1195
Roger, constable of Chester, was one of the first to use an armorial seal in England. The arms are a bend with a label of seven points, an unusually early example of a charge that came to be regularly used to distinguish – difference – the arms of members of a single family. The interlaced pattern of the counterseal may be intended as a rebus, or play on the name, Lacy.
Seal 6.3 cm, counterseal 4.2 cm (actual size).
British Library, Harley Charter 52 H.43A

completely covered by the same multiple chevrons that appeared on the Clare family's equestrian seals. In the 1190s, perhaps a little earlier, some seals instead of a mounted knight had simply a coat of arms on a shield of contemporary pattern, with the top curved and the upper corners rounded. Robert Bruce, lord of Hart and Annandale, had one with a lion above a diagonal cross (saltire); Ranulf, earl of Chester, one about 1200 with a lion rampant[9]. During the first quarter of the thirteenth century the fashion spread quickly in both England and Scotland and we find the earliest examples of two-sided seals that had a mounted rider in front and a shield of arms on the back – among them in Scotland one of Alexander son of Walter Stewart about 1226, and in England one that Hubert de Burgh, earl of Kent, was using by 1229. This was to be a persistent style – we have already seen that it was used for some of the deputed great seals of the English crown. Like the equestrian seals that they were twinned with or replaced, these heraldic seals were round and large, some 5 to 8 centimetres across. The shield now had a straighter top and pointed upper corners, and the blank space around the shield was beginning to attract ornamentation – flowering tendrils, a crouching lion or wyvern on each side, or a cusped outline with further ornament in the spandrels.

Fig 48

Fig 49

[9] T.A. Heslop, 'The Seals of the Twelfth-Century Earls of Chester', *Journal of the Chester Archaeological Society*, 71 (1991), pp.193–4.

48 Ranulf de Blundeville, earl of Chester, c.1200
The shield is of contemporary style, with the top curved and the corners rounded. The device of a lion may reflect Ranulf's descent from Henry I, but he later used a different armorial device, three wheatsheaves. This may mean that he had arms for the earldom that were different from his personal device, or it may simply have been a change of a kind possible before the rules of heraldry were fully defined.

7.2 cm (actual size).
Public Record Office, DL 27/235

49 John Warenne, earl of Surrey, c.1250
Two-sided seals, equestrian in front and armorial on the back, were used by many magnates in the thirteenth century. Here the Warenne coat of arms – checky – appears also on the horse's caparison. The shield has a straight top and pointed upper corners and instead of blank spaces around it we find eight cusps with tendrils of ivy.

8.0 cm (reduced).
British Library, Seals lxxx.66, 67

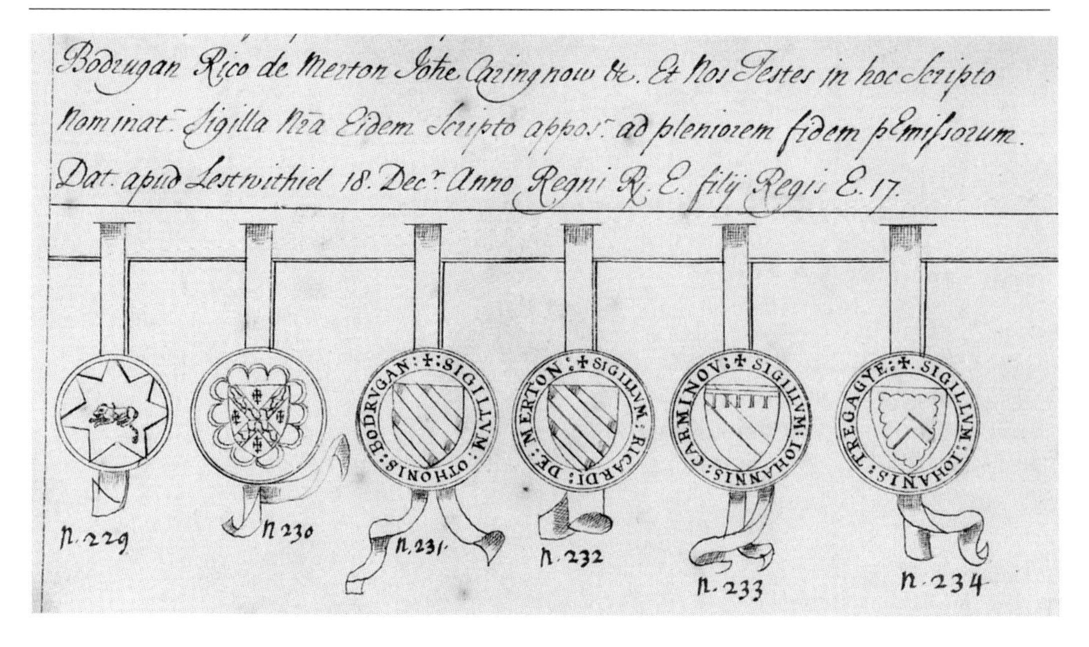

50, 51 Heraldic seals in the fourteenth century
Drawings of the seals on two documents, each originally with six seals, from the unpublished treatise 'Aspilogia' by John Anstis, Garter King of Arms 1718–44. They show how the design of small heraldic seals developed.

50 The four seals on the right are of the simple design characteristic of the thirteenth century, with blank spaces around each shield. Here, on the grant of a manor dated at Lostwithiel, Cornwall, in 1323, they may have seemed old-fashioned. Unusually, all the witnesses to this grant sealed it by way of confirmation.
British Library, Stowe MS.666, f.3v

Alongside the large heraldic seals of the aristocracy, the first half of the thirteenth century produced an ever-growing number of smaller seals, some 3 or 4 centimetres across, with shields of arms. Although the chronology is not yet clear, the fashion for armorial bearings began in the late twelfth century to spread from the aristocracy, first to their lesser kindred then to their feudal tenants and dependants, a process that gained momentum in the thirteenth century. By the middle of the century Nicholas Bat, mayor of London in 1253–4, had an armorial seal.[10] Presumably, as heraldry became systematised and ever more widely adopted, heraldic seals offered the chance of displaying rank and status in smaller – and thus cheaper – compass than was possible by the image of mounted knight or standing lady. These heraldic seals developed like the larger ones, with the same kinds of ornament around the shield – but on the smaller seals the blank spaces were less

[10] P.R. Coss, *The Knight in Medieval England 1000–1400* (Stroud, 1993), pp.79–81; J.A. Goodall, 'The Use of Armorial Bearings by London Aldermen in the Middle Ages', *Transactions of the London and Middlesex Archaeological Society*, 20 (1959–61), pp.1–5.

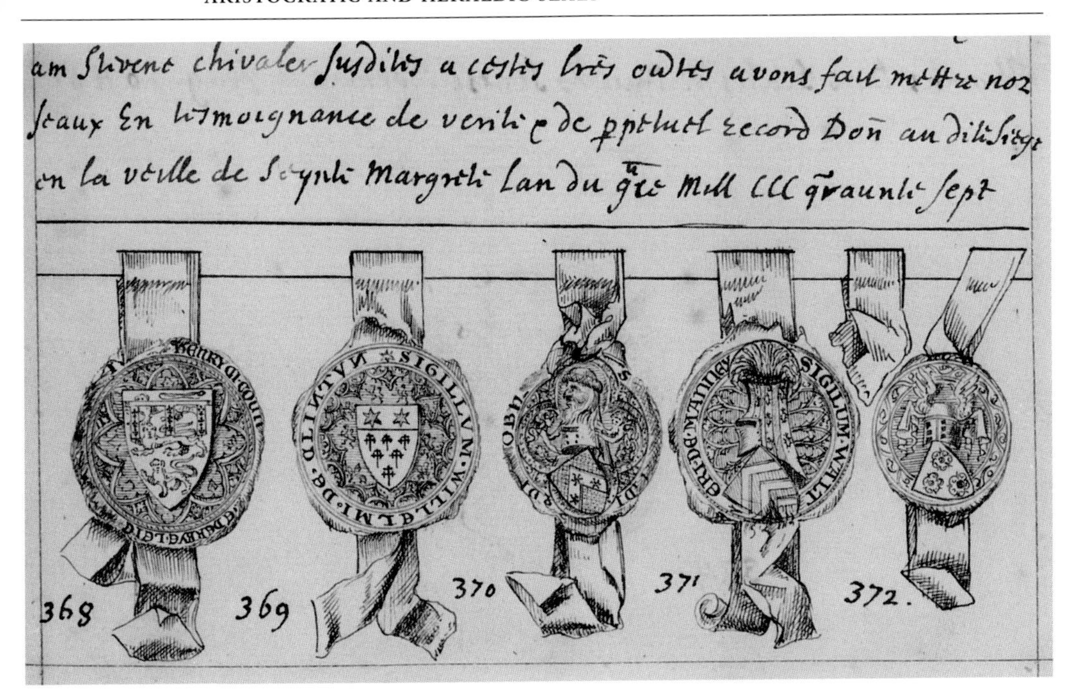

51 The five surviving seals on this document of 1347 are typical small heraldic seals of the time. The space around each shield is filled with fine tracery or other ornament and three show the shield on its side – couché – surmounted by a helm and crest. The seal at the right-hand end has tendrils in place of a legend round the edge.

British Library, Stowe MS.666, f.35r

noticeable, and by the end of the thirteenth century many still showed simply a shield of arms with no ornament of any kind.

The document known as the Barons' Letter gives an interesting picture of the seals used by upper-class Englishmen in 1301. It was a reply to the pope's claim to be feudal overlord of Scotland and it survives in two copies – in the end neither was sent to Rome. It was sealed by 7 named as earls and 96 others who had attended the parliament at Lincoln and, of the 103 seals, 95 survive on one or other copy. Among these 95 there are 14 equestrian seals, and 7 of these – 5 of them belonging to earls – are two-sided, with a shield of arms on the back. One seal has a grotesque design of human faces and animals, and all the rest are heraldic, including one that is two-sided with a shield of arms on each side.[11] As we shall see, there is reason to suppose that not every seal on the Barons' Letter was the principal seal of its owner, but all the same it points to an overwhelming preponderance of heraldic seals – the equestrian seal had all but disappeared outside the top ranks of the aristocracy.

However, in the fourteenth century the use of heraldic seals further

[11] Lord Howard de Walden, *Some Feudal Lords and their Seals MCCCJ* (privately printed, 1904).

increased. In the three classes of ancient deeds in the duchy of Lancaster's records, which come from widespread areas in England and the Welsh marches,[12] of some 1460 different personal seals on thirteenth-century documents 9 per cent are heraldic, 5 per cent equestrian and 1 per cent have figures of ladies, whereas of some 870 personal seals on fourteenth-century documents 39 per cent are heraldic and less than 1 per cent are either equestrian or ladies' seals. The proportion of heraldic seals has risen from less than one-tenth to well over one-third, and this may well be a typical English sample. The change is partly because – as we shall see – the ownership of seals by non-gentry declined; fewer people overall owned seals, and the well-to-do were a higher proportion of those who did. But probably it is due even more

52 Ralph Double, citizen and fishmonger of London, late fourteenth century
As the fashion for heraldry grew in the fourteenth century quasi-heraldic devices began to appear on the seals of persons who might not be thought entitled to bear arms. This seal names Ralph Double in the legend, and the arms on the shield are a chevron between two fish in chief and a hunting horn in base. This impression dates from 1380.
2.3 cm (enlarged).
Public Record Office, C 148/58

to the spread of heraldry throughout the gentry – in the mid-fourteenth century many people had coats of arms whose predecessors a hundred years earlier did not. Some assumed the arms of their superior lords, in the words of Camden's *Remains* 'borrowing from their Lords Armes of whom they held in fee, or to whom they were most devoted'.[13] Members of knightly families who were not themselves knights might use the family arms on a seal; an example is Sir John Langley's younger brother Robert, who had been given the manor of Wolfhamcote, Warwickshire, from the family estates and who in 1317 was using a seal with his brother's arms.[14] In 1292 in England the Statute of Arms ruled that esquires could display only the arms of their knightly masters – they could not assume arms of their own.[15] This is clear evidence that some had already done so, and in any case this need not preclude their using heraldic seals even if the arms were not personal to themselves. In fact esquires were soon using their own arms – Sir Robert Laton's roll of arms of about 1370 specifically included the arms of esquires along with those of 'kings, princes, dukes, earls, barons and lords and knights'.[16] Some men ranking as esquires were using seals with their own

12 P.R.O. DL 25, DL 26, DL 27.
13 W. Camden, *Remaines concerning Britaine*, ed. J. Philpot (5th edn, London, 1636), p.209.
14 N. Saul, *Knights and Esquires: the Gloucestershire Gentry in the Fourteenth Century* (Oxford, 1981), p.21.
15 *Statutes of the Realm* (Record Commission; 11v., 1810–28), i, pp.230–1; its date is discussed by N. Denholm-Young, *Collected Papers* (Cardiff, 1969), pp.110–13.
16 A.R. Wagner, *A Catalogue of English Medieval Rolls of Arms* (Society of Antiquaries, Aspilogia 1; 1950), p.65.

arms in the 1320s, and P.R. Coss has recently shown how the custom spread among such families in one Warwickshire parish, Tanworth in Arden, during the fourteenth century.[17]

No one has ever tried to categorise the heraldic seals that proliferated in the fourteenth and fifteenth centuries. There was great variety of size, style and design – and indeed workmanship, though the general level was high – but they seem to have developed the same way throughout Britain. Some common trends were already visible by the end of the thirteenth century. The

53 John Davidson of Newlands, Peeblesshire, c.1536
The form of heraldic seals established by the late thirteenth century continued to the sixteenth century and later, but there was latterly great variety in style and pattern. This is an unusually simple late example. The arms are a stag with an arrow through its neck and a cinquefoil below.
2.9 cm (enlarged).
British Library, Seal xlvii.1993

54 Edmund Beaufort, duke of Somerset, c.1448
A fine example of a late-medieval magnate's seal. The shield, couché, is supported by an eagle and a tiger and is surmounted by a helm with mantling and a lion as a crest. On the shield are the Beaufort family arms, quarterly France and England with a bordure. Somerset was governor of Normandy for the king, and this was his seal for the town of Bayeux.
6.3 cm (actual size).
British Library, Seal xlvii.1630

smaller heraldic seals were getting smaller still – 2 centimetres across or even less – and by the mid-fourteenth century we seldom find blank spaces around the shield of arms. One convention which originated in the thirteenth century and became common in the fourteenth was to show the shield hanging from a tree which would appear above, often reduced to three vestigial branches or bushes. The shield was often placed in an outline of cusps and

Figs 50, 51

[17] P.R. Coss, 'Knights, Esquires and the Origins of Social Gradation in England', *Transactions of the Royal Historical Society*, 6th Ser. 5 (1995).

angles – its shape presented a challenge to neat composition – with complicated tracery in the spandrels. Throughout the fourteenth century the design of heraldic seals became ever more elaborate, and their engravers exercised both ingenuity and imagination in their settings for the coats of arms. From the mid-fourteenth century both men's and women's seals might show not one but several coats of arms, sometimes with the owner's at the centre surrounded by those of related families. On the larger seals of the aristocracy – and size of seal still went hand in hand with rank – heraldic development affected the design. One seal of the Barons' Letter of 1301 – the seal of Henry, earl of Lancaster and Leicester – shows the shield set on one side (couché) with helmet and crest above and a beast on either side.[18] Many later seals of the nobility were in this style, but perhaps because it tended to emphasise crest, mantling and supporters at the expense of the shield it became less widespread in the fifteenth century.

Fig 54

OTHER SEALS OF LAY MAGNATES

Some magnates' seals from the mid-twelfth century onwards had counterseals impressed on the back. This may mean that these important people had responsible clerks who kept their seals for them and that the counterseal, the magnate's small private seal that he carried always with him, was added as a guarantee that the document was sealed with his assent. It seems likely that this is why counterseals were used regularly by, for instance, Ranulf, earl of Chester (1181–1232) from about 1218,[19] or by successive earls of Dunbar throughout the thirteenth century. However, usage varied. Of three twelfth-century families known to have had household clerks, the earls of Gloucester used counterseals, the Mowbrays did not and the earls of Devon began to use them only in the early thirteenth century,[20] while an alternative arrangement is suggested by the seals of Hugh, Ranulf's predecessor as earl of Chester (1153–81), which have counterseals with the names certainly of William Barbedavril and probably of other clerks who wrote or issued the charters.[21] But we cannot suppose that a counterseal always implies a household on this scale. When, say, Ralph Musard of Derbyshire impressed counterseal as well as seal in the 1220s, this was probably simply because it was seen as a dignified or customary thing to do, strengthening the authority of the seal itself.

Fig 47

At first these counterseals were mostly engraved gems, presumably worn in rings, with a surrounding legend that named the owner. The signets of Richard I and Llywelyn ap Iorwerth exactly fit this pattern. On Llywelyn's the legend reads 'Sigillum secretum Lewlini', and we find increasingly in the thirteenth century that *secretum* appears in the legend and that the owner's

Figs 24, 30

[18] Lord Howard de Walden, *Some Feudal Lords*, p.29.

[19] Heslop, 'Seals of the Earls of Chester', p.195.

[20] *Earldom of Gloucester Charters*, pp.24–30; D.E. Greenway (ed.), *Charters of the Honour of Mowbray* (British Academy, Records of Social and Economic History, new ser. 1; 1972, pp.lxvi–lxx, lxxxii–lxxxiv; *Charters of the Redvers Family*, pp.39, 41, 51.

[21] Heslop, 'Seals of the Earls of Chester', pp.187–92.

name is omitted. This of course meant that the seal could pass unchanged from one head of family to the next; earlier, Isabel, countess of Gloucester (c.1189–1217), had used her father's small seal, a gem with an eagle in its design, with the legend altered from 'Aquila sum et custos comitis' (I am the eagle and guardian of the earl) to 'Ego sum aquila custos domine mee' (I am the eagle, guardian of my lady).[22] Now, however, the gems began to be replaced by heraldic counterseals of about the same size or slightly larger, some 2 or 3 centimetres across. An early example was used in 1218 by Gilbert de Clare, earl of Gloucester and Hertford, on the back of his equestrian seal – a simple shield of arms, with the legend 'Sigillum Gileberti de Clara'. By the mid-thirteenth century these heraldic counterseals were widespread, without wholly replacing the engraved gems – the fourth earl of Dunbar (1182–1232) used a gem with anonymous legend, the fifth earl (1232–48) a shield of arms with his name on it, the sixth earl (1248–89) an anonymous shield of arms, and the seventh earl (1289–1308) once more an anonymous gem. The legends on the last two are 'Sigillum amoris' (seal of love) and 'Je su sel de amur lel' (I am the seal of loyal love) – the aristocracy was uninhibited in using seals with the same legends as anyone else, legends that might seem trite or banal. An unusual alternative to a shield of arms was a miniature mounted knight or standing lady; examples are the seal, with no legend at all, that Peter de Montfort of Beaudesert, Warwickshire, put on the back of his larger heraldic seal, and the seal of Margaret Basset of Quorndon, Leicestershire, inscribed simply 'Sigillum secretum'.

Fig 40

The surviving impression of Margaret Basset's seal is not a counterseal but authenticates by itself a grant of property at Quorndon. We know the small private seals of magnates through their use as counterseals because these are on the formal charters that are most likely to survive, but this cannot have been their chief function – mostly they would be used by themselves to authenticate many less important documents or messages. The distinction between large formal seal and small private seal may have seemed less clearcut to contemporaries than it does to us, and it is likely that the small heraldic seals that became so common in the course of the thirteenth century took their origin in the private seals of the great. In looking at other kinds of seal we shall see how changes in their style and design might be influenced or anticipated by subsidiary seals; and subsidiary seals as a whole deserve more serious attention than they have commonly received – they were often the vanguard, not the stragglers, in sigillographic development.

The Barons' Letter of 1301 is interesting in this connection. It was dated at Lincoln on 12 February, following a parliament there for which writs of expenses (effectively permission to leave) had been issued on 30 January. Nearly all those who sealed the letter were at the parliament and many, perhaps most, probably stayed on in Lincoln – like the king himself – and were able to attach their seals there, but we know that more than a few had already gone home, for an official was sent on extensive journeys with the two copies of the letter for them to seal.[23] We cannot thus be certain who

22 *Earldom of Gloucester Charters*, p.24.

23 Cf. F.M. Powicke, *The Thirteenth Century* (Oxford, 1953), p.705.

55 The Declaration of Arbroath, 1320
This letter from the Scottish earls and barons asked the pope to persuade Edward II to recognise the freedom of the nation of the Scots. Some fifty seals were affixed, mostly at one time but eleven were added later. Less than half of the seals survive, but these show that the seals were intended to be in the order of the names on the document, the first half in red wax, the second half in green.
Scottish Record Office, SP 13/7

sealed at Lincoln. Roger Bigod, earl of Norfolk, used a small, certainly private, seal with a shield of arms and Philip de Kyme an anonymous heraldic seal that he is known to have used also as a counterseal. We may reasonably suspect that several others were not their owners' primary seals – Sir Roger de Scales used an heraldic seal with no legend, Thomas de la Roche a tiny shield-shaped one.[24] Some of the greatest magnates may have had their administrative staff – and their formal seals – with them at Lincoln. But it looks as if some of the rest had left their seals at home, guilty of what the legal treatise attributed to Henry Bracton had castigated as 'inexperience or negligence, as where he had delivered his seal to his steward, or his wife, when it ought to be guarded more carefully'.[25] All the same, they all had on their persons the means of authenticating the letter, and their private seals were regarded as fully valid, even for this most formal purpose. Detailed sigillographic comparison of the Barons' Letter with the Declaration of Arbroath of 1320 would be interesting and instructive. This was another letter to the pope from barons of the realm – this time of Scotland – whose seals were attached at a single operation but who were probably not all present in person: two sent their heirs to represent them, and others simply sent a seal, among them David de Brechin who, perhaps fearful of letting his own seal out of his hands, sent his wife's instead.[26]

Fig 55

On the whole, though, it is the magnates' lack of duplicate seals, or of seals for special purposes, that is surprising. In the fourteenth and fifteenth centuries counterseals came to be used only by the greatest magnates, and only seldom by them – the counterseal with sacred monogram used by the earl of Douglas in 1418, the heraldic counterseal of the duke of Bedford in 1429 are examples, but they are exceptional. So too is the implication in the legend of a seal used by William, Lord Hastings, in 1477 – 'Sigillum armorum' – that he had more than one seal in concurrent use. He may simply have had also a signet ring; in 1400 all Scottish tenants-in-chief were required to have seals – explicitly not just signets – of their own and in 1429 it was ruled that a freeholder unable to attend the sheriff's court should send someone in his place 'with the sele of his armys', but by 1469 a sheriff might return writs under either seal or signet.[27] In 1439 the earl of Dunbar's signet, attached to an indenture, was said to have 'the force and the effect of his seele'.[28] Long before, however, in 1262 the future Edward I had to borrow the seal of one of his knights when writing to his father, the king, because his own seal was being used for business in London; he had no special seals for his lordships of Chester and the Channel Islands, and documents there were authenticated

[24] Lord Howard de Walden, *Some Feudal Lords*, pp.15, 133, 134, 147.

[25] G.E. Woodbine and S.E. Thorne (eds), *Bracton De legibus et consuetudinibus Angliae* (Cambridge, Mass., 4v., 1968–77), iv, p.236.

[26] A.A.M. Duncan, 'The Making of the Declaration of Arbroath', in D.A. Bullough and R.L. Storey (eds), *The Study of Medieval Records: Essays in Honour of Kathleen Major* (Oxford, 1971), pp.181–7.

[27] *The Acts of the Parliament of Scotland* (Record Commission; 12v., 1814–75), i, p.575; ii, pp.19, 95.

[28] ibid., ii, p.55.

by the personal seals of the local justiciars and bailiffs.[29] The lordship of Chester acquired its own seals – both a great seal and a privy seal for the earl – only in the fourteenth century, as it became more closely linked to the heir to the throne and to the crown itself: the Chester chamberlain's account enters no fees from sealing in 1302 but some £4 in 1359–60.[30] The English crown in fact seems to have been more willing to proliferate seals in its administration than other owners of estates and lordships. A special seal made for the duchy of Lancaster's chancery at Monmouth under Edward IV falls into this pattern, and though there are references to the chancery seal of another marcher lordship, Wentlooge (Gwynllwg) and Newport, when it belonged to Hugh, earl of Stafford (1372–86), this again seems quite exceptional.[31] The often complex administration of large landed estates was conducted without special seals – stewards and bailiffs used their own personal seals and had no seals of office.

[29] J.R. Studd, 'The Seals of the Lord Edward', *Antiquaries Journal*, 58 (1978), pp.310, 314–15.

[30] P.H.W. Booth, *The Financial Administration of the Lordship and County of Chester 1272–1377* (Chetham Society, 3rd ser. 28; 1981), pp.13, 50, 63, 69.

[31] W.S. Walford and A. Way, 'Examples of Mediaeval Seals', *Archaeological Journal*, 14 (1857), pp.55–7; T. Wakeman, 'On the Chancery of Monmouth', *Journal of the British Archaeological Association*, 14 (1858), pp.56–60; D.H. Williams, *Catalogue of Seals in the National Museum of Wales* (Cardiff, in progress, 1993–), i, p.25.

4 SEALS OF THE SECULAR CLERGY

BISHOPS' SEALS OF DIGNITY

The principal seals of bishops – sometimes called their seals of dignity – developed a distinctive form quite different from that of lay magnates, and they typify the pattern of seals of other higher clergy and ecclesiastial officials.[1] This form emerged at the beginning of the twelfth century. We have seen how the seal-matrix of one bishop – Aethelwold, bishop of East Anglia in the mid-ninth century – survives from before the Norman Conquest. Its circular impression, 3.5 centimetres across, has at its centre an eight-pointed star. Post-Conquest bishops' seals are radically different. The two-sided seal of Odo, bishop of Bayeux – one of the three seals mentioned in Domesday Book – is an oval probably about 7.5 centimetres high and 5 centimetres wide, and in front it shows the bishop standing, vested for Mass, raising one hand in benediction and holding a crosier (pastoral staff or crook) in the other. This is similar to some other bishops' seals from northern France at this time, except that they do not show the figure full-length. However, Odo in England was earl of Kent, and the back of his seal departs dramatically from French models, showing him on horseback, wielding what may be a staff but looks very like a sword – a design clearly copied from the seal of his half-brother, King William I. It was in fact very seldom that a bishop had a two-sided seal.[2]

Fig 2

Fig 21

The round seal of Wulfstan, bishop of Worcester (1062–95), shows him with crosier and book, sitting on a throne, and a few other early bishops' seals also show the figure seated – the round seal of Alexander at Lincoln (1123–48) and the seals of Peter at Chester (1075–85) and Simon at Worcester (1125–50), both pointed ovals. Two other contemporary bishops' seals – of Osbern at Exeter (1072–1103) and Gundulf at Rochester (1077–1108) – seem to be modelled on Odo's in showing a standing vested figure, with crosier and hand raised in benediction; Gundulf's is round, Osbern's a tall, almost pointed, oval. Anselm, archbishop of Canterbury (1093–1109), had a seal that combined elements from several of these precursors – a broad oval showing him standing vested, holding a book in one hand and managing with the other both to hold a crosier and to give a blessing.[3] Others had

Fig 56

Fig 57

1 Much of what follows on bishops' seals draws on W.H. St John Hope, 'The Seals of English Bishops', *Proceedings of the Society of Antiquaries*, 2nd ser. 11 (1886–7), pp.271–306.

2 T.A. Heslop, 'English Seals from the Mid Ninth Century to 1100', *Journal of the British Archaeological Association*, 133 (1980), pp.10–12.

3 ibid., pp.11–13; J. Cherry, 'The lead seal matrix of Peter bishop of Chester', *Antiquaries Journal*, 65 (1985), pp. 472–3.

56 Osbern, bishop of Exeter, 1072–87
One of the earliest surviving seals of an English bishop. Like the seal of Odo, bishop of Bayeux (fig.21), it shows the bishop standing with a crosier in his left hand and the right raised in benediction. He wears mass vestments but no mitre or dalmatic. The halo around the head suggests that the design and shape of the seal may derive from a figure of Christ or the Virgin.

7.5 × 4.8 cm (actual size).
British Library, Doubleday Cast D 17

57 Anselm, archbishop of Canterbury, 1093–1103
Anselm's seal combines elements from earlier bishops' seals. Its shape is a broad oval, and though he is shown standing he holds both the open book and the crosier of earlier seated figures, as well as giving a blessing.

7.8 × 6.7 cm (actual size).
British Library, Campbell Charter vii.5

similar seals, but pointed ovals and without the book, among them Ranulf Flambard at Durham (1099–1128), the first Richard de Belmeis at London (1108–27) and – the earliest known seal of a Scottish bishop – Robert at St Andrews (1127–59). On all these the bishop is bareheaded, and it may well have been Anselm's successor at Canterbury, Ralph d'Escures (1114–22), who was first shown wearing a mitre, achieving what was to be the standard form of bishops' seals for over two hundred years: a pointed oval, showing a

Fig 58 full-length standing figure, vested, mitred, with crosier in the left hand and the right raised in benediction. The first bishop's seal to survive from Wales – of Nicholas ap Gurgant at Llandaff (1148–83) – is among the many of this type.[4]

There was only occasional departure from this pattern – most notably a group of Scottish bishops' seals in the first half of the thirteenth century that showed the figure facing half-right instead of full-face – but it underwent increasing elaboration. The earliest of these seals contained large vacant

58 Hugh Balsham, bishop of Ely, 1257
The design is typical of bishops' seals of dignity in the twelfth and thirteenth centuries: a standing figure wearing dalmatic and mitre, holding a crosier in the left hand and blessing with the right. However, the double line of beading between the legend and figure is unusual, and 'H II' has been placed in the field because this was the second bishop of Ely named Hugh – at this date the legend did not give the bishop's surname.
7.2 × 4.8 cm (actual size).
British Library, Seal lv.31

spaces around the effigy, which were gradually filled with various types of decoration. A first step in this direction was the seal of Richard of Dover, archbishop of Canterbury (1174–84), which covers the whole field with lattice-work. But from the mid-twelfth century subsidiary elements began to be added on either side of the central effigy, or even above or below it. These elements include stars, church buildings, a hand holding a cross, symbols of saints – as the keys of St Peter at Winchester – or even engraved gems set into the seal-matrix – of the four on the seal of Archbishop Boniface of Savoy at *Fig 59* Canterbury (1244–70) one bore the head of Jupiter Serapis. A fashion for the heads of saints in sunken panels on each side was begun on the seal of Richard Grant (or Wethershed) at Canterbury (1229–31). These appeared too in Scotland, on the seal of Alan, bishop of Argyll (1253–62), but in England they rapidly developed to half-length figures, then to full-length, *Fig 60* which first appear on the seal of Walter Giffard, archbishop of York (1266–79). St Peter and St Paul are there set in canopied niches; traces of a canopy over the central figure had first appeared on the seal of Nicholas

[4] D.H. Williams, 'Catalogue of Welsh Ecclesiastical Seals as known down to 1600 A.D. Part I: Episcopal Seals', *Archaeologia Cambrensis*, 133 (1984), p.116.

59 Boniface of Savoy, archbishop of Canterbury, 1245
In the thirteenth century decorative elements were placed in the space beside the figure on bishops' seals, but the insertion of four engraved gems into this matrix is unique. On one is the head of Jupiter Serapis, identifying the Roman god with an Egyptian one. Below the figure is a representation of, presumably, Canterbury Cathedral.
8.3 × 4.7 cm (actual size).
British Library, Doubleday Cast E 142

60 Walter Giffard, archbishop of York, 1266
The full-length figures of St Paul and St Peter beside the bishop are an innovation. Earlier, however, the heads, then half-length figures, of saints had appeared here on bishops' seals in place of purely decorative elements. The canopies over the saints foreshadow the elaborate architectural designs of later seals.
8.2 × 5.2 cm (actual size).
British Library, Seal lix.11

Farnham at Durham (1241–9) and side-shafts were occasionally added. From the early fourteenth century canopies and side-shafts became normal, bringing the central figure and flanking saints into a single composition. One of the finest examples, which introduced new features from French seals, belonged to a bishop of Durham, Richard of Bury (1334–45); his second seal shows enormous architectural complexity, housing no fewer than eleven

Fig 61

standing figures and creating a fine illusion of a third dimension.[5] As far as we can tell from surviving seals, this development of an architectural setting occurred at about the same time in both Scotland and England, but rather later in Wales.

Other less obvious changes in the seals have wider implications for ecclesiastical or social history. There were changes in the bishops' vestments. *Fig 57* Anselm's was the first seal to show the bishop wearing a dalmatic. When mitres first appear on the seals they were worn – to modern eyes – sideways,

61 Richard of Bury, bishop of Durham, 1334–5
This new seal replaced the bishop's first seal of dignity within a year of his consecration and it may have been a gift from abroad. Certainly the antecedents of its design are French, and in England it set a new fashion for bishops' seals: the figure stands in a shaped niche, with elaborate architectural surrounds which house eleven saints and add depth to the composition.
8.9 × 5.7 cm (actual size).
Dean and Chapter of Durham, 3.9 Pont.6a

so that the division between the two horns could be seen from the front. Hugh du Puiset at Durham (1153–95) is the first bishop shown with the mitre's flat side in front, Hugh de Nonant at Coventry and Lichfield (1188–98) perhaps the last with it the other way round. Starting with Geoffrey Ludham at York (1258–65) almost every archbishop of York or Canterbury is shown carrying a cross in place of a crosier. The legend on successive seals of William Fraser at St Andrews (1280–97) has a double interest: it harks back to the seals of his predecessors before 1254 in calling him bishop of the Scots (*episcopus Scottorum*), not of St Andrews, and it is also the first to give a bishop's surname – the earliest English example is William of Wykeham at Winchester (1367–1404), and it became usual only in the fifteenth century.

[5] T.A. Heslop, 'The Episcopal Seals of Richard of Bury', in N. Coldstream and P. Draper (eds), *Medieval Art and Architecture at Durham Cathedral* (British Archaeological Association, Conference Transactions, 3; 1980), pp.156–8.

62 Anthony Bek, bishop of Durham, 1284
This is the only two-sided seal of dignity of a medieval bishop from Britain. In front it shows him seated, like a king enthroned, flanked by St Oswald and St Cuthbert in niches, and his vestments are embroidered with a cross with splayed ends (cross moline), his personal coat of arms. On the back is the Coronation of the Virgin with the bishop below, kneeling in adoration – the first seal of dignity to depict a suppliant bishop below a saint or religious scene.
8.5 × 5.7 cm (enlarged).
British Library, Seals xlvii.232, 233

Heraldry first appears in the second half of the thirteenth century. There are shields of arms beside or below the figures on the seals of William Fraser at St Andrews (1280–97), Matthew de Crambeth at Dunkeld (1288–1309) and David Martin at St Davids (1293–1328). An early example from England is the seal of Anthony Bek at Durham (1284–1311), a seal remarkable in several ways. It is two-sided and on the front Bek is not standing but seated, like a king enthroned, flanked by Durham's two powerful saints, Oswald and Cuthbert, and his vestments are embroidered with a cross with splayed ends, a cross moline, his personal coat of arms. There is no other instance from medieval Britain of a two-sided bishop's seal of dignity, and not many late-medieval seals where the bishop is shown seated – though John Grandisson at Exeter (1327–69) and Thomas Cheriton at Bangor (1436–47) are examples. However, from the end of the thirteenth century heraldic devices – usually shields of arms, of the kingdom, of the see or of the bishop himself – appear regularly on bishops' seals.

Fig 62

63 Robert Lancaster, bishop of St Asaph, 1411
This is typical of many fifteenth-century episcopal seals. The principal figures, in canopied niches, are saints, here St Peter, the Virgin and Child, and St Paul. Below, under an arch, is the bishop, shown half-length, in prayer. On either side of him hangs a shield of arms, on the left two keys crossed, for the see of St Asaph, and on the right three hands with nail-marks.
7.5 × 4.9 cm (actual size).
British Library, Seal xxxvii.50

The back of Anthony Bek's seal was just as innovative. It shows the Coronation of the Virgin with the bishop below, kneeling in adoration – the first seal of dignity in a completely new style, which took a saint or religious scene as its principal subject, with the bishop himself shown as a suppliant figure below. There are only a few other examples before the 1350s – among them John de Pilmor, bishop of Moray (1326–62), who had on his seal the Trinity with the emblems of the evangelists – but from the late fourteenth century onwards this became the usual design for a bishop's seal of dignity, almost wholly supplanting the standing figure of the bishop.

Fig 63

OTHER EPISCOPAL SEALS

When a bishop died his seal-matrix was often ceremonially broken. At Durham the pieces of the seal would be solemnly offered at the shrine of St Cuthbert; a silver-gilt chalice was then made from Richard of Bury's four seals in 1345, and from the seals of Thomas Hatfield in 1381 a silver-gilt image of the bishop that was hung at the end of the saint's shrine.[6] Richard of Bury's four seals will have included the palatinate seal that was peculiar to Durham, but any bishop will have owned more than one seal.

The seal of dignity was to the bishop what the great seal was to the king – it was used for the most important official documents. It was kept by the chaplain or clerk who was responsible for writing the bishop's formal acts and letters – he might indeed be called keeper of the seal (*custos sigilli*) and in the twelfth century a single chancellor might keep the seals of both the

[6] C.H. Hunter Blair, 'A Note upon Mediaeval Seals with Special Reference to those in Durham Treasury', *Archaeologia Aeliana*, 3rd ser. 17 (1920), pp.254–5.

bishop and the cathedral chapter.[7] The bishop himself had a private seal for his own use and at first this was often used as a counterseal to the seal of dignity, to guarantee authenticity as a safeguard against fraudulent use. Usually it was an engraved gem, presumably worn in a ring. The earliest dated example was used by Theobald of Bec at Canterbury in 1144, but Henry of Blois at Winchester (1129–71) may have used his earlier; from Scotland the earliest known was used in 1158 by Arnold, two years before he became bishop of St Andrews, and the first from Wales are two used by

64 Private seal of Walter Giffard, archbishop of York, 1266–79
Bishops used engraved gems as counterseals less in the thirteenth century than in the twelfth, but two are known that belonged to Walter Giffard. This gem shows Fortune holding a shield in one hand, a winged figure of Victory in the other, but its thirteenth-century setting bears Christian wording, 'Ave Maria gracia plena'. Giffard's other private seal with a gem bore the heads of St Peter and St Paul.
4.1 × 2.5 cm (enlarged).
British Library, Seal lix.10

William Saltmarsh at Llandaff (1186–91).[8] Some of these gems were of wildly unsuitable design: Thomas Becket at Canterbury (1162–70) had an antique intaglio showing Mercury or Mars, naked except for a helmet, Hugh de Nonant at Coventry and Lichfield (1188–98) one engraved 'Allah' in Arabic, and Robert Wishart at Glasgow (1273–1316) used one with a nymph adjusting her footwear while supporting herself with one hand on a giant phallus. Some gems had legends that gave a Christian persona to a pagan subject – one used by Roger de Pont l'Évêque at York (1154–81) had a grotesque head with three faces but was inscribed 'Caput nostrum Trinitas est' (our head is the Trinity). Later, however, the gems in bishops' signet rings were more often engraved with allegorical or Christian motifs; thus at Winchester William of Wykeham (1367–1404) had a griffin with its prey, William Waynflete (1447–86) Christ with Mary Magdalene.

Fig 64

We know less of these private seals of bishops after the twelfth century because they were no longer used as counterseals to the seals of dignity. They were replaced by subsidiary official seals that now began to appear – when

[7] C.R. Cheney, *English Bishops' Chanceries 1100–1250* (Manchester, 1950), pp. 33, 38, 40, 42; K. Edwards, *The English Secular Cathedrals in the Middle Ages* (2nd edn, Manchester, 1967), pp. 177, 205.

[8] Williams, 'Catalogue of Welsh Ecclesiastical Seals. Part I', pp.116–17.

used alone they were the equivalent of the king's privy seal or signet. In appearance these fall into several clearly defined types, but in our present state of knowledge we cannot safely assign them to particular functions. We do not know enough about late-medieval bishops' chanceries – or, less grandiosely, their arrangements for writing and issuing letters of all kinds – and,

65 Subsidiary seal of William of Bondington, bishop of Glasgow, c.1233
St Kentigern, patron of Glasgow Cathedral, standing in mass vestments and holding a crosier, blesses the bishop who kneels before him with head bowed. The design of a saint with suppliant figure was used on bishops' subsidiary seals long before it appeared on their principal seals, the seals of dignity. The subsidiary seal was used with the seal of dignity as a counterseal, but also by itself to seal less formal documents.

5.1 × 2.9 cm (enlarged).
British Library, Seal xlvii.251

as with royal seals, the word *secretum* is used ambiguously. There seems, at best, to be some inconsistency in the use of these subsidiary seals – nor, indeed, should we expect to find uniformity among sees as diverse as, say, York and St Davids, or Moray and Winchester. They were certainly used at first as counterseals to the seals of dignity, though by the end of the fourteenth century bishops throughout Britain had stopped countersealing. But primarily they were used by themselves to authenticate less formal, less permanent, less important documents than the seals of dignity. Detailed analysis of their use might throw new light on the way bishops ran their sees in the late middle ages.

The earliest subsidiary seals were pointed ovals, some simply reduced versions of the seals of dignity. Most seals of dignity were from 6 to 9 centimetres high, 3.5 to 5.5 centimetres wide; there seems to have been no general change in their size between the twelfth century and the sixteenth, but the richer sees perhaps tended to have the larger seals. The subsidiary seals might measure up to 6 by 4 centimetres or even more. In view of this, and of inconsistency in their use, it is not always clear whether a particular seal is a subsidiary seal or a seal of dignity. Thus, because the few known specimens are on a chronologically ordered sequence of documents, we are invited to see four pointed-oval seals of Robert Wishart at Glasgow

(1273–1316) as four successive primary seals; from their size and design, however, we might reasonably suppose that only the second and fourth were seals of dignity, the other two subsidiary ones. The designs of bishops' subsidiary seals are in fact of especial interest because they anticipate change in the seals of dignity. Some of the earliest – such as that of Geoffrey of

66 Seal *ad causas* of Richard of Bury, bishop of Durham, c.1335
Though it was by a different engraver, working in England, this seal shows the immediate influence of the bishop's second seal of dignity (fig.61) in the shaped backs of the niches and the elaborate architectural detail. The seated figures are the Virgin and Child and St Cuthbert, patron of Durham; below, the bishop prays in adoration and at the top is a lion.
5.7 × 3.8 cm (enlarged).
British Library, Seal liv.76

Henlaw at St Davids (1203–14) – show the bishop standing as on his seal of dignity and with similar legend. Others have figures of saints, like a seal of Walter de Gray at York (1215–55), showing St Peter and St Paul with the legend 'Orate pro nobis sancti dei apostoli' (pray for us, holy apostles of God), and on some of these the bishop appears in prayer at the base, long before this convention appeared on seals of dignity. A seal of William of Bondington at Glasgow (1233–58), showing the bishop kneeling beside St Kentigern, may be seen as a precursor of this; the seal of Walter Cantilupe at Worcester (1237–66) shows the Coronation of the Virgin with the bishop beneath.

Fig 65

From the early fourteenth century some of these pointed-oval seals had in the legend 'sigillum ad causas' or just the word *cause* in another context – as on the seal of Thomas Arundel at Ely (1374–88), 'Dum causas audis absit collusio fraudis' (when you hear cases may there be no conspiracy to deceive). These seals were large, scarcely smaller than the seals of dignity, and were probably for business of only slightly less importance. John of

Fig 66

Lindsay at Glasgow (1333–c.1335) had an *ad causas* seal, but in Scotland their place was probably taken by the bishops' round seals, sometimes called *sigillum rotundum* in the legend, which appear in the fifteenth century – at St Andrews by 1433, for instance, in Argyll by 1439. Here again there are difficulties in identifying these seals because after 1427 the seals of dignity of the bishops of Glasgow were, exceptionally, also round, showing St Kentigern and shields of arms, and this style may occasionally have been copied in other Scottish sees.

Fig 67

Richard at Bangor (1237–67) had a pointed-oval seal called *sigillum privatum* in its legend, Richard Kellaw at Durham (1311–16) was among others who had one called *secretum* – but this was more usual in a different group of

67 *Sigillum rotundum* of James Kennedy, bishop of St Andrews, c.1440
In fifteenth-century Scotland many bishops, besides the seal of dignity, had a round seal – *sigillum rotundum*, sometimes so called in the legend. This was probably used in place of a seal *ad causas* for less important documents. Here, below the martyrdom of St Andrew, is a shield bearing the Kennedy family arms, within a royal tressure, supported by two angels.
3.6 cm (enlarged).
British Library, Seal xlvii.374

episcopal seals of the fourteenth and fifteenth centuries. These were round in England, oval in Scotland, from 2.5 to 6 centimetres across, some showing a saint but mostly showing the bishop's arms – indeed Henry Beaufort's at Winchester (1405–47) calls itself *sigillum armorum*. The functions of the pointed-oval subsidiary seals of the thirteenth century may have come to be divided between the more formal seals *ad causas* (whether or not so called in the legend) and these less formal *secreta* – but this can be only a guess.

OTHER CLERICAL SEALS

In 1237 the papal legate Otto, in a council at London, issued constitutions for the government of the English church. One paragraph dealt with seals. Not only archbishops and bishops should have seals but also their officials, as well as abbots, priors, deans, archdeacons and their officials, rural deans, cathedral chapters and other colleges and convents. To be their recognised seal (*sigillum auctenticum*) it should always name the institution or office and also the holder of any office held permanently; for a temporary appointment, such as a rural dean, the office alone should be named, so that the seal

68 Dunwich rural deanery, fourteenth century
No individual is named in the legend, and the seal is clearly a seal of office, to be used by successive rural deans; this impression dates from 1356. On board the one-masted ship are St Andrew and St Peter, identified both by a diagonal cross and a key and by 'And'' and 'Petr'' engraved above them.
3.6 × 2.3 cm (enlarged).
British Library, Harley Charter 83 C.51

69 Archdeacon of Cardigan, c.1292
Seals of lesser church dignitaries followed a pattern broadly similar to bishops' seals though smaller in size. Thus they are usually a pointed oval, by the late thirteenth century showing a saint – here the Virgin and Child – with suppliant figure below. The legend on this seal does not name the archdeacon but gives his initial, W.
4.5 × 2.8 cm (enlarged).
British Library, Doubleday Cast F 40

could be passed from one holder to the next.[9]

How far this ruling affected practice has never been investigated. We catch a distant echo of its phraseology on the seal of dignity of Bishop William Elphinstone at Aberdeen (1488–1514), called *sigillum autenticum* in its legend – but bishops' seals were of course the norm long before 1237. On the seals of secular clergy other than bishops little systematic work has been done – and even the seals of bishops' officials, commissaries-general and vicars-general, which can be seen as deputed seals of the bishops themselves, have never been analysed as a group. We can say that nearly all official clerical seals were pointed ovals, and that their designs broadly reflect the seals of the bishops. But the details – the chronology of their introduction

[9] F.M. Powicke and C.R. Cheney (eds), *Councils and Synods with other Documents relating to the English Church II: A.D.1205–1313* (Oxford, 1964), i, pp. 257–8, quoted in full in J.P. Dalton, *The Archiepiscopal and Deputed Seals of York* (Borthwick Texts and Calendars, 17; York, 1992), pp. 14–15.

and of successive changes in design and legend – all need investigation. One difficulty is that probably far fewer seals survive of lesser clergy than of bishops, being used on less important documents and less likely to be carefully kept. W.H. St John Hope in 1893 knew of only 66 seals of the 2200 archdeacons who held office in England and Wales between 1066 and 1540; more have come to light since he wrote, and some must still be undiscovered, but the proportion surviving must be small, and the same is no less true of the seals of rural deans – D.H. Williams has found only four from the whole of Wales.[10]

A few seals of twelfth-century archdeacons have varied designs: the dove above Noah's ark at Huntingdon (1155–84), an eagle at Llandaff (c.1170–80). But most show the archdeacon standing – seated at York in 1138 – nearly always with a book, and in the course of the thirteenth century the design changed in the same way as bishops' seals of dignity: other elements appeared on either side – sheaves at Chester in 1252 – and a canopy was added. It is interesting that the figure was usually vested as a deacon – even in the mid-fourteenth century, though by then archdeacons had long been in priest's orders. However, from the end of the thirteenth century most archdeacons' seals show the Virgin and Child or a saint, with suppliant figure below. Some fifteenth-century archdeacons in England and Scotland used what are simply heraldic personal seals, quite outside the clerical tradition.[11] In this the archdeacons were aligning themselves with lesser clergy. The seals of parish priests seem indistinguishable from those of their parishioners in shape, size and design, though some late-medieval personal seals showing a saint and suppliant figure may have belonged to clergy rather than laymen. On the whole, though, it seems as if distinctively clerical seals had clear connotations of ecclesiastical rank and dignity – they were not used by the clergy as a whole.

Fig 69

10 W.H. St John Hope, 'The Seals of Archdeacons', *Proceedings of the Society of Antiquaries*, 2nd ser. 15 (1893–5), p.27; D.H. Williams, 'Catalogue of Welsh Ecclesiastical Seals as known down to 1600 A.D. Part II: Seals of Ecclesiastical Jurisdiction', *Archaeologia Cambrensis*, 134 (1985), pp.181–7.

11 St John Hope, 'Seals of Archdeacons', pp.27–31.

70 Non-heraldic personal seals, 1260
Seals of freeholders of Charwelton, Northamptonshire, four of the nine attached to an agreement over pasture rights with the next village, Byfield. Their designs are typical of mid-thirteenth-century non-heraldic seals – a fleur-de-lis, a flower, the Lamb of God – and each names its owner in the legend. The largest, at the right-hand end, is less than 3 cm across, significantly smaller than earlier seals of this kind (fig.71).
British Library, Harley Charter 84 D.56

5 NON-HERALDIC PERSONAL SEALS

THE SEAL-OWNING PUBLIC

'It was not the custom in the past for every petty knight to have a seal. They are appropriate for kings and great men only'. This comment by Richard de Lucy, chief justiciar of England, was made in a law-suit before Henry II, probably in the 1160s.[1] By the end of the century seal-ownership in England had spread even further beyond what he deemed acceptable – but this was the result not of social pretension but of legal necessity. The growing insistence, apparently led by the monasteries, on a written document to confirm every transfer of rights in freely held land combined probably with rapid growth in the land market to produce a vastly increased number of charters of conveyance – and every grantor of a charter had to attest it with a seal. This explosive spread of the use of seals meant that by the early thirteenth century probably as many individuals in England were using seals as at any time in the next three hundred years; they comprised everyone who had free land or other properties to convey or other business to be agreed in formal writing.

This included even the smallest landholders. Between 1217 and 1232 fifty-six tenants in Butterwick and Frieston in Lincolnshire made an agreement with Ranulf, earl of Chester and Lincoln, over feudal rights; every one attached a seal to the document.[2] Nor were villeins – those of unfree legal status – in practice barred from owning seals. They might hold free land, which would be conveyed by charter, and although such documents do not name the parties' legal status it has been demonstrated that some late-thirteenth-century agreements with Gloucester Abbey were sealed by villeins.[3] The so-called Statute of Exeter in 1285, laying down procedures for inquiries into coroners' conduct of office, required that any unfree man who served as a juror should – like the free man – have a seal to confirm the written presentment.[4] A late-twelfth-century poem tells of the Norfolk peasants who, celebrating the sealed charter their lord had given to free them from villeinage, used the wax to make a candle when it got dark[5] – but this is in the context of many crazy things done by the peculiarly witless people of

[1] E. Searle (ed.), *The Chronicle of Battle Abbey* (Oxford, 1980), pp.214–15.

[2] P.R.O. DL 27/270, reproduced in *Guide to Seals in the Public Record Office* (2nd edn, London, 1968), pl.II.

[3] R.H. Hilton, *The English Peasantry in the Later Middle Ages* (Oxford, 1975), pp.153–5.

[4] *The Statutes of the Realm* (Record Commission; 11v., 1810–28), i, pp.210–11.

[5] T. Wright (ed.), *Early Mysteries, and other Latin Poems of the Twelfth and Thirteenth Centuries* (London, 1844), pp.xxi, 94–5.

Norfolk, and all other evidence suggests that the peasants even there would already be as fully aware as their betters of the significance of a seal on a document.

In looking at non-heraldic personal seals we are looking at the seals of most seal-users. They include the seals used by peasants, and reference is sometimes made to peasant seals – but this may be misleading, for no particular feature of design or style has yet been found to distinguish their seals from those of artisans, clerics, traders or anyone else. The people who used the seals discussed in other chapters are more or less closely defined: officials of the crown, the higher clergy, the lay upper classes, corporate bodies of one sort or another. Those who used the seals discussed here cannot be limited in this way. We distinguished upper-class seals primarily by their design – equestrian seals, heraldic seals, seals showing standing ladies – and this was justifiable in that only the aristocracy and gentry used seals of these types. But the spread of heraldry in the fourteenth century brought these distinctively upper-class seals within the purview of a wider range of the gentry, whose predecessors, no less socially eligible, had used other sorts of seal – and in any case, as we have seen from their counterseals, from the mid-twelfth century even the highest aristocracy had used other seals as well. In discussing personal seals that show neither mounted riders nor standing ladies nor coats of arms we are not dealing exclusively with the humbler levels of society. Again, for their personal seals the various officials of church and monastery, town and government, often had heraldic seals – but not necessarily. If the signet ring identified as Richard I's did not name the king – or if it had lost its legend – it would have been among the seals to be considered in this chapter.

We are in fact discussing here some four-fifths of all seals surviving from medieval Britain. They have been far less studied than the other one-fifth. It is the sheer volume of these personal seals that most hampers any historical investigation of them, and it is only relatively recently that historians have started to ask basic questions about their manufacture, their ownership and their usage. Guides to the subject are few. They are almost entirely excluded from the most comprehensive catalogues of British seals – Birch's *Catalogue of Seals in the Department of Manuscripts in the British Museum* includes only those used as counterseals and a few from Scotland, and there are not many in the classes of document covered by Ellis's *Catalogue of Seals in the Public Record Office*. The catalogue of seals in Durham Cathedral archives by Hunter Blair is exceptional in providing an extensive list from a large and important collection – but the personal seals are mostly from north-east England only. It is partly because no printed source offers an overall conspectus that so little analytical work has been done on personal seals. We know nothing of their regional variations in design, of where the matrices were made or by whom. We cannot associate particular styles of seal with particular social or economic groups – beyond what is obvious, that the more elaborate, finely engraved seals must have belonged to the well-to-do. We cannot exactly date any of the successive changes in style and usage that we observe. For England and Wales we can draw a general outline of the way these seals developed, of the broad changes that occurred in the course of time – though in many places our picture badly needs the precision that future research may supply. For Scotland we cannot even do this, and rather than attempt an account that would be largely guesswork it seems best to leave Scottish seals altogether out of consideration in this chapter. Scottish seals could easily have been brought in as illustrations, or used as examples of some particular development – but this would risk falsifying the picture, for what was typical and widespread in England may have been far from typical in Scotland. The best service that can be done here for the study of these personal seals from Scotland is to set out the present state of knowledge of their development in England and Wales; this will at least serve as a point of reference with which the Scottish seals can be compared or contrasted. We might reasonably expect their history to differ in the two countries. In particular we might suppose that in Scotland, instead of the sudden rapid adoption of seals that occurred in late-twelfth-century England, there was a more gradual extension of their use over some two centuries, from the upper classes downwards – but this is no more than a guess that may well be proved wrong.

In England the rapid adoption of seals owed much to the local land market – which may itself have been a new phenomenon or which may merely now have begun to use written charters to confirm its transactions. More knowledge of this local land market – and it is a topic of current research – could throw light on when and how seals came into general use. We might learn much of later developments from research into the law regarding seals, especially the case-law accessible to us mainly through the year-books. But the primary need, in England and Wales as in Scotland, is for more analytical work on the seals themselves, their form and their use.

BEFORE 1300

From what centre or centres the use of seals spread in late-twelfth-century England we do not know – nor exactly when or at what rate. The seals themselves were nearly all round and typically some 3.5 to 4 centimetres across. In some, probably the earliest style, no line separated the legend round the edge from the design. The legend began with a cross and the word 'Sigillum ...' which was followed by the owner's name in Latin in the genitive case. The design would be a simple image, engraved so as to leave much of the field blank. In all this the seal of Peter Corbucion is typical – and typical too in its relatively crude but vigorous engraving of a lion and in the uneven letters of the legend, with the N reversed. A walking bird, a fleur-de-lis, an elaborate tendril, were among other designs no less typical than the lion. In the early thirteenth century – and again we can be no more precise – this style was modified. Seals became smaller – perhaps 3 centimetres wide. A line now always separated the legend from the design, and the design occupied more of the field, leaving less blank space. Shape started to become more varied and the pointed oval, hitherto rare among these seals, become much more common, especially for women – two-thirds of the seals owned

Fig 71

Fig 70

71 Peter Corbucion of Studley, Warwickshire, late twelfth century
The seals that began to be used by humbler people in the late twelfth century were quite large but had simple designs engraved with large blank areas around. Here there is a line between the design and the legend; this is lacking on what are probably the earliest seals of this kind.
4.5 cm (enlarged).
Public Record Office, E 329/122

by women in one sample were pointed ovals, but only one-tenth of those owned by men.[6]

It was seals of this style that predominated throughout the thirteenth century, with legend simply naming the owner. There was a tendency for them to get slightly smaller in the course of time and for the designs to become more elaborate – but extremely simple designs were still common at the end of the century. There was in fact great variety of subject, though some were especially common, above all the fleur-de-lis – sometimes inverted – in many different forms, but also a star or cross with varying number of points, sun and crescent, a flower seen full-face or the whole plant seen from the side, an arrangement of ears of corn (or perhaps conifer branches), a bird, a fish, a lion walking or rampant, and many more. Sometimes the design specifically relates to the owner. An artisan might have a design reflecting his trade, such as the seals of Gilbert, butcher of Durham, with a chopper or axe, and Eustace, brewer of Ferryhill, county Durham, which shows a man mashing at a high tub with six hoops. Some designs were canting references or rebuses playing on the owner's name. Thus John le Gaunter had a glove on his seal, though he was a chaplain from Newcastle-upon-Tyne, not a glovemaker; Imania Orchard had three trees.[7] The reference might be more obscure. In the 1220s and 1230s Henry Beck of Lusby in Lincolnshire was using seals showing a cross with splayed ends, a cross moline – a design which a grander relative was already using as an heraldic device and which may have been viewed as a general family symbol, whether heraldic or not.[8]

Fig 72
Fig 73

6 S.E. Rigold, 'Two Common Species of Medieval Seal-Matrix', *Antiquaries Journal*, 57 (1977), p.324.

7 D.C.D. 4.3 Spec.26, 2.16 Spec.35, 40 (Hunter Blair, 1061, 1919).

8 P.R.O. DL 25/2929, 2930, 2931; the device occurs on the equestrian seal of Walter Beck, c.1210, DL 27/282 (Ellis, P1009).

72, 73 Seals of tradesmen in County Durham, late thirteenth century
Many artisans' seals had wholly conventional designs, but on some the design referred to their trade – a tailor, for instance, might have a pair of scissors – as on these two examples.

72 Gilbert, butcher of Durham, had a simple chopper or axe on his seal.

2.8 × 1.8 cm (enlarged).
Dean and Chapter of Durham, 2.14 Spec.36

73 The seal of Eustace, brewer of Ferryhill, shows a man wearing a long gown with hood thrown back, mashing at a high tub with six hoops.

3.1 × 2.2 cm (enlarged).
Dean and Chapter of Durham, 4.12 Spec.3

Seals of Jews are a small but interesting group. Of five known, only one is distinctively Jewish, the seal of Bonefay son of Barton of Nottingham, which shows the tablets of the law and gives his name in Hebrew, though written from left to right following Latin usage. That we have so few seals of Jews must be partly because they were accustomed to authenticating even Latin documents by their sign manual in Hebrew – but probably also because, since they were barred from holding land in feudal tenure, most of their transactions concerned money, not landed property, and the relevant records thus had little permanent value, especially after all Jews were expelled from England in 1290.[9] It is a reminder that the seals that survive to the present day may not be a fair sample of those that were actually impressed in the middle ages.

Fig 74

The finest seals were engraved by goldsmiths – but we know practically nothing of the engravers who produced the matrices for the vast mass of these personal seals. It is interesting that there is a mistake in the Hebrew legend of Bonefay son of Barton's seal, and its design too shows nothing of the competence that we would expect had it been made by a Jewish gold-

[9] D.M. Friedenberg, *Medieval Jewish Seals from Europe* (Detroit, 1987), pp.43–58.

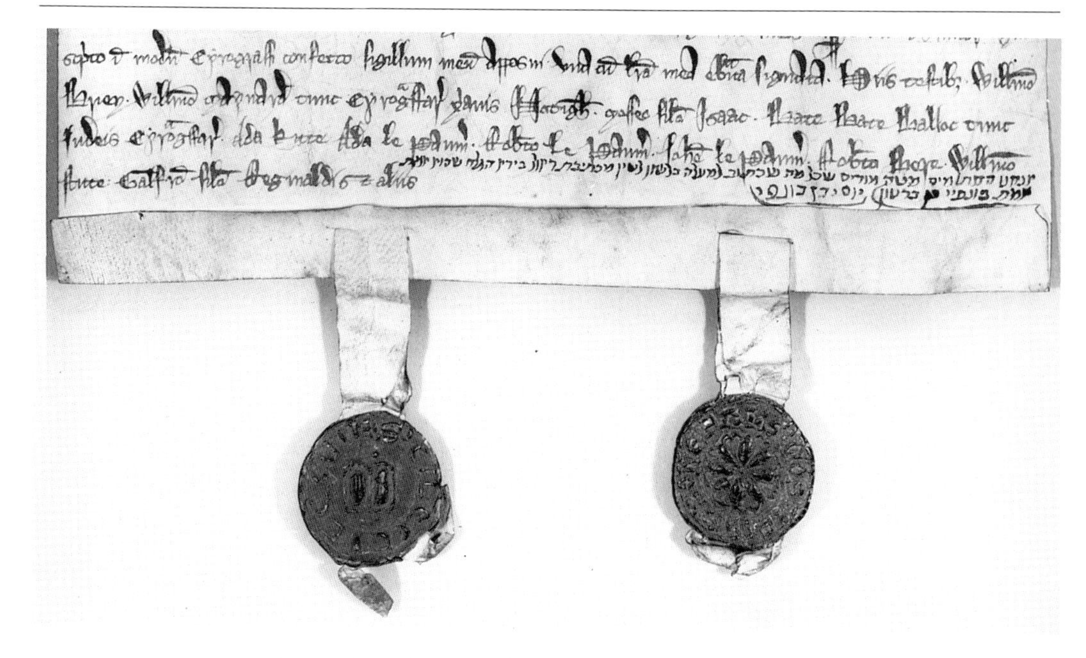

74 Jewish seals, mid- or late thirteenth century
These are attached to the grant of a property in Nottingham by Bonefay son of Barton and Yosi, his son – at the end of the Latin document is a confirmatory note in Hebrew. On Yosi's seal, on the right, is a conventional eight-petaled flower, and the legend, giving his name, is in Latin. On Bonefay's seal, on the left, are the tablets of the law and his name is in Hebrew, engraved badly and probably not by a Jew. It is the only seal known from medieval Britain with Hebrew legend.
Both 2.4 cm.
Westminster Abbey muniments, 6374

smith. Seal-engravers' work was indeed sometimes ignorant or careless. The letters N and S are often engraved back to front – though less frequently in the course of the thirteenth century. Names may be miscopied. Even so usual a name as John appears not as 'Iohannis' but 'Lohannis' – it may even be 'Lomnnis' – on the seal of John son of Peter of Wyham in Lincolnshire. *Fig 75* Benedict Garnet, a Lancashire forest-keeper with bow and hunting-horn on his seal, appears in its legend as 'Gervet', an example of the common misreading of u for n in contemporary handwriting.[10] The engraver of the seal of Richard son of Martin of Skidbrooke in Lincolnshire, running out of space as he engraved 'Martini', added a diagonal stroke between T and I to make N, and added another I at the end.[11] An alternative way out of this difficulty, found on some seals, would be to put the legend's final letters in the field of the central design.[12] Most seals, certainly, are neat and carefully made. But of all the seals surviving from medieval Britain only a tiny proportion displays fine craftsmanship or artistry.

10 P.R.O. DL 25/1213.
11 P.R.O. DL 25/2971.
12 E.g. P.R.O. LR 14/1154.

75 Seal with miscopied legend, mid- or late thirteenth century
On this seal of John son of Peter of Wyham, Lincolnshire, his name in the legend has been engraved as 'Lohannis' – even perhaps 'Lomnnis' – instead of 'Iohannis'. Ordinary personal seals in the thirteenth century, probably produced locally, were often engraved with little craftsmanship or care.
3.2 × 1.8 cm (enlarged).
Public Record Office, DL 25/3055

When John son of John, a wineseller, gave a house in Beverley to Rievaulx Abbey he attached the seal of his lord because he had no seal of his own.[13] At this time – the late twelfth century – having no seal was a not uncommon predicament; two grants of land to Rufford Abbey, Nottinghamshire, bear wax impressed with a key instead of a seal, and in a third the grantor, because he had no seal, explicitly used his wife's key for the purpose.[14] But from the early thirteenth century this problem seldom arose, and we can link this change with another aspect of thirteenth-century seals: sometimes seals attached to a charter are so alike in size, shape and style that they must have been produced by the same engraver. Often they are seals of husband and wife or of others who might reasonably be expected to have seals made together. But sometimes they are of people apparently unconnected except by taking part in the particular transaction, and we must suppose that the seals were made especially for this act of sealing. This would probably be at the expense of the recipient of the grant, who will have had the written charter drawn up to confirm it – and this in turn throws light on another phenomenon, the fact that it was not unusual for an individual to own more than one seal. These seals were not designed for different purposes like the formal seal and privy seal of the magnate – sometimes one, sometimes another would be used to authenticate documents in the same way. A possible explanation is that provision of a seal hardened into a custom, so that a grantor expected a seal to be supplied, even if already a seal-owner.[15] Some seals of a single owner have the same design. Alice of Eden, who had property at Durham, had two seals, one round and one a pointed oval, but both

Fig 76
Fig 77
Fig 78

13 J.C. Atkinson (ed.), *Cartularium abbathie de Rievalle* (Surtees Society, vol.83; 1889), p.84.

14 C.J. Holdsworth (ed.), *Rufford Charters* (Thoroton Society; 4v., 1972–81), ii, pp.413–14; iii, pp.492, 530.

15 P.D.A. Harvey, 'Personal Seals in Thirteenth-Century England', in I. Wood and G.A. Loud (eds), *Church and Chronicle in the Middle Ages: Essays presented to John Taylor* (London, 1991), pp.124–7.

76 Henry of Bishopthorpe and his wife, Matilda, mid- or late thirteenth century
Although her seal names Matilda only as the daughter of Osbert, the document – concerning property at Welton, Lincolnshire – shows that she was Henry's wife. The two seals are exactly alike in shape, size, style of engraving and form of the legend, differing only in the design. Almost certainly they were made together as a pair for husband and wife.

Both 3.7 × 2.4 cm (enlarged).
Public Record Office, DL 25/3089

Fig 79

with a fleur-de-lis;[16] Thomas of Hurtmore from Surrey had three, each with a stag's head on it.[17] On the other hand, William son of Osbert of Saltfleetby in Lincolnshire had a five-petalled flower on one of his seals, a five-pointed star on another and a fleur-de-lis on a third,[18] and sometimes we find uniformity of design not between the seals of a single seal-owner but between the seals of different owners on a single charter – like one that has three seals with a cartwheel, one with six spokes, one with seven and one with eight.[19] If the recipient of the grant provided the seal, the grantor may or may not have been allowed to select the design.

Even though anyone authenticating a document in the thirteenth century would normally own a seal, other persons' seals might still occasionally be attached to confirm or strengthen the seal of the party to the transaction. Normally this would be explained in the document itself – the further seal

[16] D.C.D. 3.17 Spec.7, 8 (Hunter Blair, 835, 836).
[17] P.R.O. E 210/3559, E 326/4018, E 326/4013.
[18] P.R.O. DL 25/2670, 2807, 2864.
[19] P.R.O. DL 25/2422.

77 Three seals by a single engraver, 1219–29
These three seals on a grant to Margam Abbey, Glamorgan, are so alike in shape, size and quality of engraving that they were probably made by a single engraver for this particular transaction – this would not be unusual. More remarkable is that, as their legends show, there was a single seal for each of two groups of brothers among the grantors – on the left is the seal of the sons of Wasmihangel (four are named in the grant), in the centre the seal of the sons of Ruathlan (two are named).
All three 4.2 cm (actual size).
British Library, Harley Charter 75 D.16

78 Two seals of Peter Gall of Saltfleetby, Lincolnshire, mid-thirteenth century
These seals are from different matrices but one was probably copied from the other. Both have the same shaped central stem of the fleur-de-lis, the same lines on the inside of its branches, the same spelling of the surname, 'Gl'', in the legend – and, taken together, these are too distinctive to result from chance. We can only guess why and how so many people owned duplicate seals at this time.
Left 3.5 × 2.9 cm, right 3.2 × 2.8 cm (enlarged).
Public Record Office, DL 25/2635, 2774

was added 'since our seals are not known to you', 'for greater security', or similar phrase. The added seal might belong to a feudal overlord, a cleric, an official of some kind or, as we shall see, a corporate body, and the practice continued throughout the middle ages. The lord of the manor, Reginald de Punchardon, added his seal when, at some date before 1230, Walter son of Hubert le English conveyed some 10 acres to a fellow-landholder in Ellingham, Hampshire; when Walter Romsey transferred the patronage of Maiden Bradley Priory, Wiltshire, in 1422, his small anonymous seal was

79 Two seals of Thomas of Hurtmore, mid-thirteenth century
Thomas of Hurtmore in Godalming, Surrey, used at least three seal matrices, each naming him in the legend and each with a stag's head as the design. One possibility is that in granting land by sealed charter he was provided with a new seal by the grantee and chose the same design each time.
Left 3.6 × 2.5 cm, right 2.9 × 2.0 cm (enlarged).
Public Record Office, E 210/3559, E 326/4018

supported by the heraldic seals of his three 'much feared lords', the earls of March, Devon and Salisbury; a grant of property in Preston, Lancashire, in 1443, bore the supporting seals not only of the mayor but of seven other individuals, all specified in the document.[20] It was not only obscure people who confirmed their documents in this way. The founder of a chantry at Childrey, Berkshire, in 1368 had his charter sealed by the bishop of Salisbury 'because the seal of Edmund Childrey is to many unknown' – yet he was a sergeant-at-law who a few years later became a justice of the king's bench.[21] It is unlikely that these confirmatory seals were provided free of charge. In

[20] S.F. Hockey (ed.), *The Beaulieu Cartulary* (Southampton Records Series, vol.17; 1974), pp.94–5; L.C. Loyd and D.M. Stenton (eds), *Sir Christopher Hatton's Book of Seals* (Oxford, 1950), p.21; P.R.O. DL 25/1167.

[21] *Calendar of Close Rolls 1364–8*, p.463.

the late twelfth century Roger de Mowbray and his son Nigel gave Byland Abbey in Yorkshire access to the seals of themselves and their heirs without paying a fee.[22] The rarity of such a grant implies not that such fees were seldom charged but rather that they were seldom remitted.

'The man who acknowledges a seal to be his, acknowledges the ink and parchment attached to the seal to be his deed' – a dictum produced in a case before royal justices at the beginning of the fourteenth century.[23] One's seal was thus a valuable possession and its loss a serious matter. In the words of one medieval Scottish text, 'There are two things that everyone ought to guard carefully, that is his tongue and his seal'.[24] As William Dugdale later put it, 'so tender was every man in those times, of his Seal, that in case he accidentally had lost it, care was taken to publish the same, least another might make use of it to his detriment'. In 1241 the loss of Bartholomew Petch's square seal (*sigillum meum quadratum*) while in someone else's keeping was reported to the king and recorded on chancery's close rolls; in 1270 it was proclaimed in the king's bench that Benedict de Haugham's seal, with a head in the centre below his name, was henceforth of no validity, whoever now held it.[25] On the other hand, according to the mid-thirteenth century treatise on English law ascribed to Bracton, if someone's charter had been read in public and named the witnesses 'it is not of great importance whether it is sealed with his own seal or another's' – a dictum repeated in two slightly later treatises, Britton and Fleta.[26] Remembering how the Statute of Exeter looked for jurors who owned seals, it seems as if two different lines of thought on the matter were current in thirteenth-century England. Certainly we sometimes find that a document bears another person's seal, without explanation or comment. Often it is the seal of someone closely related. Bertram of Durham uses the seal of his mother, Emma, on a charter of 1229, and rather later in the thirteenth century Rose, widow of John Smith of Pleshey, Essex, attached to her charter what it calls 'my seal' but is actually the seal of John Smith himself.[27] But sometimes it is the seal of someone apparently unconnected. Roger son of William of Moorcroft used the seal of Hugh de Frodsham in a charter from Lancashire; a Berkshire charter of Alice de la Hill and her son Walter in 1274 has only one surviving seal, but the name on it, partly illegible, is Richard —y.[28] Against this background it is unsurprising that anonymous seals, without the owner's name, had started

22 D.E. Greenway (ed.), *Charters of the Honour of Mowbray 1107–1191* (British Academy, Records of Social and Economic History, new ser. vol.1; 1972), pp.49–50, 54.

23 B.L. Additional MS. 35116, f.267v (the manuscript is a contemporary compilation of pleas); we are grateful to Dr P.A. Brand for kindly giving us this reference and translation.

24 *The Acts of the Parliament of Scotland* (Record Commission; 12v., 1814–75), i, p.736.

25 W. Dugdale, *The Antiquities of Warwickshire*, ed. W. Thomas (London, 2v., 1730), ii, p.922; *Close Rolls 1237–42*, p.345.

26 G.E. Woodbine and S.E. Thorne (eds), *Bracton De legibus et consuetudinibus Angliae* (Cambridge, Mass., 4v., 1968–77), ii, p.120; F.M. Nichols (ed.), *Britton* (Oxford, 2v., 1865), i, p.257; H.G. Richardson and G.O. Sayles (eds), *Fleta*, vol.3 (Selden Society, vol.89; 1972), p.31.

27 D.C.D. 4.16 Spec.120 (Hunter Blair, 977); P.R.O. DL 25/1443.

28 P.R.O. DL 25/594, 1380.

to come into general use before the end of the thirteenth century.

They seem to have evolved from the privy seals of the aristocracy and higher clergy. Often the privy seal was an engraved gem, probably worn in a signet ring, and these in particular sometimes omitted the owner's name from the legend, reading simply 'Sigillum secreti' – those of William Percy about 1200 and William of Lancaster between 1220 and 1246 are examples.[29] Others have legends showing that the privy seal might close as well as authenticate a private letter: 'Lecta cela nec revela' (what you read conceal, and do not reveal) or – one belonging to William son of William of Ashford – 'Cela segreta Willelmi' (hide William's secrets).[30] Seals of this kind that are neither gems nor, apparently, their owners' secondary, privy seals can be found in the 1250s. It is difficult to gauge their spread exactly, because most private charters are undated before about 1270, but from the 1270s and 1280s a trickle of such seals turns into a stream. From the beginning of the fourteenth century they rapidly became the predominant type of non-heraldic seal.[31]

80 Anonymous: bird of prey, fourteenth century
The legend is one often found: 'Frange lege tege' (break, read, conceal) – a reminder that the seal would be used not just to authenticate a formal document but also to close a private letter. The crude engraving is typical of many late-medieval anonymous seals.
2.2 cm (enlarged).
British Museum, Department of Medieval and Later Antiquities, 1987–4–3 13

AFTER 1300

These seals changed at the end of the thirteenth century in other ways besides omitting the owner's name. They became progressively smaller – round ones, still the most common, came to be no more than some 1 to 1.5 centimetres across or even less. Designs became more elaborate and imaginative and the legend might now be in French or English instead of Latin. Sometimes the legend referred to the seal's role in closing a private letter – 'Prive su' (I am private), 'Frange lege tege' (break, read, conceal) and others. Sometimes it was a pious phrase – 'Timete deum' (fear God), 'Ave Maria' (hail, Mary). But often it referred directly to the design, and legend and design combined allowed wider expression of individual taste. Wit, sentimentality and popular devotion all appear, and some motifs recur over and over again.

Fig 80

[29] P.R.O. DL 27/83 (Ellis, P1867), DL 25/578.
[30] P.R.O. E 42/493, E 212/68 (Ellis, P910, P956).
[31] Harvey, 'Personal Seals', pp.120–2.

81 *Left* Anonymous: hare riding on hound, early fourteenth century
The only legend on this seal is 'I ride' engraved at the top. The hunting satire was a popular theme on anonymous personal seals, often with the hunting call 'Sohou' in the legend. Though seals were still mostly round or pointed ovals, their shape was becoming more varied and this seal, from an impression of 1316, is shield-shaped, perhaps reflecting the spread of shields of arms beyond the ranks of knights.
2.0 × 1.5 cm (enlarged).
Public Record Office, E 329/299

82 *Right* Anonymous: hawk and duck, fourteenth century
The hawk with its prey, a duck or rabbit, often appears on anonymous seals, usually with the legend that is on this example, 'Alas je su pris' (alas, I am caught) – the meaning is amatory. The use of French and English legends instead of Latin gave freer scope for wit and for play on words.
1.8 cm (enlarged).
Public Record Office, E 213/315

These include scenes with animals: the hare riding on a hound and blowing a hunting-horn with 'Sohou' (a hunting cry) or 'I ride', the sleeping lion with 'Wake me no man', the squirrel eating a nut with 'I crake notis' (symbolising sexual conquest),[32] the hawk taking a duck, rabbit or other prey with 'Alas je su pris' (alas, I am caught), the grotesque with 'Je su nul tel' (there is none like me). They include a man and a woman or just their heads or two crossed hands with legends such as 'Je su sel de amur lel' (I am the seal of loyal love), 'Love me and I the' and 'Lel ami avet' (you have a loyal friend) – or, by way of contrast, 'Bi the rode wimen ar wode' (by the rood, women are mad). They include too religious motifs: the Lamb of God with 'Agnus dei', the Virgin and Child with 'Mater dei memento mei' (Mother of God remember me), the head of John the Baptist with 'Caput Johannis'.

Fig 81
Fig 82
Fig 83
Fig 84
Figs 85, 86

But there was great variety in design and legend, and whereas many seals were of stock patterns and must have been bought ready made others were clearly made to order. These may include some of unusual design, with or without a forename in the legend, that could well be making some personal allusion, now lost. An example, used by Alan le Charman at the end of the thirteenth century, shows a dog and a hare gaming, with 'Hasard thin hod is

[32] M. Jones, 'Folklore Motifs in Late Medieval Art III: Erotic Animal Imagery', *Folklore*, 102 (1991), pp.199–201.

83, 84 Anonymous: love and loyalty seals, fourteenth century
Examples of designs that are sentimental rather than witty and have been termed love and loyalty seals. They often show clasped hands or a heart or, as here, a man and woman with a flowering plant between them. Legends are usually in English or French.

83 *Left* The legend here is typical of seals of this sort, 'Love me and I the'.
1.9 cm (enlarged).
British Museum, Department of Medieval and Later Antiquities, Seal-Die no.739

84 *Right* Less typical is the legend here, 'Bi the rode wimen ar wode' (by the rood, women are mad).
2.2 cm (enlarged).
British Museum, Department of Medieval and Later Antiquities, Seal-Die no.762

min'; another, of Walter of Grendon in 1335, shows the moon and a man with a bundle of thorns and a dog – the man in the moon – with 'Cur spinas Phebo gero te Waltere docebo' (I shall teach you, Walter, why I am carrying thorns from the sun);[33] yet another shows a cat eating a mouse with 'Gret wel Gibbe oure cat', which was used in 1392 by Gilbert Stone, clerk. Some which must have been specially made play cleverly on the owner's name. The seal that Thomas of Fishburn used in 1316 shows a hare above a fish with a stream or burn below – or perhaps the hare is 'borne' by the fish – though as its legend reads 'Her is no more bot a fische and har' we may wonder whether it was not originally made for someone named Fisher; one used by John Bowes in 1443 has the head of an ox (Latin *bos*) with 'Bull not I' in a scroll from its mouth.[34] Nor, indeed, did non-heraldic seals with the owner's name cease to be made – but they were vastly outnumbered by the anonymous seals, and even by the seals bearing coats of arms.

Fig 16

Not only were seals without names entirely normal from the late thirteenth century onwards; by this time any inhibitions over using another person's seal were forgotten. The clerks who wrote the documents must have owned a variety of seals that they would produce for their clients' use, for we find the same seal on deeds that have different signatories but are

[33] P.R.O. DL 25/1684, E 329/16 (Ellis, P348; cf. T.A. Heslop in J. Alexander and P. Binski (eds), *Age of Chivalry* (London, 1987), pp.116–17).

[34] P.R.O. E 43/561 (Ellis, P1397; cf. Heslop in *Age of Chivalry*, p.116), LR 14/496.

85 Anonymous: pelican in its piety, fourteenth century
The pelican in its piety, feeding its young with the blood dropping from its own breast, was a symbol of Christ's sacrifice and was one of several religious motifs popular on late-medieval anonymous seals – the legend here is 'Timete deum' (fear God). Others included the Virgin and Child, the Lamb of God and the head of John the Baptist.
2.7 × 1.7 cm (enlarged).
British Museum, Department of Medieval and Later Antiquities, 1987–4–3 15

written in the same hand. An example is an anonymous seal which appears on documents written on two consecutive days in 1465, first as the seal of William Bernard, then as the seal of Felicia Wood.[35] Where a document is sealed by several persons, it is not uncommon to find the same seal doing service more than once. One bond of 1340 has twelve seals; they include two impressions of each of three seals, all anonymous, and of the other six four are anonymous, one is an heraldic seal with a name that does not appear in the bond and only one seal bears the name – and also the arms – of a signatory.[36]

Fig 16

Now it was generally accepted that one need not have one's own seal in order to authenticate a document, it is likely that the proportion of seal-owners in the population declined – and that there were more seals in use in the thirteenth century than later in the middle ages. Those who did own seals were presumably people who would need to authenticate writings more than just occasionally. Where a husband and wife seal a document the husband is the more likely to have a seal identifiably his own, the wife an anonymous

86 Anonymous: Christ and evangelists, fourteenth century
This is more carefully and elaborately engraved than many anonymous seals of the time. Christ is seated on a throne with arms ending in dragons' heads; surrounding the central lozenge are four compartments containing the symbols of the evangelists. The legend is simply 'Iesus nazarenus' (Jesus of Nazareth). It was used by Thomas Rainham, a London goldsmith, in 1369 and he may well have made the seal himself.
3.0 × 2.2 cm (enlarged).
Public Record Office, C 148/5

35 P.R.O. DL 25/1104, 1105, 1106.
36 P.R.O. DL 25/1016.

87 Seal with a merchant's mark, fourteenth century
Some merchant's marks are difficult to distinguish from coats of arms, as they include the shape of a shield. Here, the cross at the top with its shaft splayed (within the shield outline) and the ring (in the shield, top right) are characteristic of merchant's marks. The legend names the seal's owner as W. Tore, but in this impression of 1359 it was used by Roger Harris.
2.2 cm (enlarged).
Public Record Office, E 329/235

seal; even Olive, wife of Nicholas of Littleton, a London goldsmith, provides an example of this in a document of 1319, though by 1321 she too had a seal with her name on it.[37] What kinds of people owned or used particular kinds of seal has never been explored, though the results would be of some interest if they pointed to differences between town and country, north and south or different occupations. Clerks and chaplains were perhaps more likely than others to use seals with a religious motif – but this is no more than an unquantified impression. Those whose seals were specially made were presumably the well-to-do, and seals that were clearly made to order were on the whole more carefully and finely engraved than the non-heraldic seals of the thirteenth century. The same cannot be said of the vast mass of anonymous seals, whether ready-made or not. Some legends are unintelligible even when they can be read clearly from a surviving matrix or a superb impression. The seal-engraver's workmanship might be quite as bad as in the thirteenth century or even worse. Because they are often difficult to read and it can be helpful to know what to expect, a list is given in the appendix of legends found on anonymous seals in a few wide-ranging collections.

Two distinctive seal designs were common in the fourteenth and fifteenth centuries. One was the merchant's mark, found increasingly from the late thirteenth century onwards. It was probably used only by townsmen, at least at first – the only design that we can firmly associate with a particular group of users – but this has never been formally demonstrated. The merchant's mark evolved presumably as a sign for marking goods and achieved the status of a non-heraldic personal symbol. Even so, it was not jealously guarded. In 1330 William Sire, burgess of Newcastle-upon-Tyne, seems to have borrowed the seal, with name and merchant's mark, of his fellow-burgess, John of Alnwick, who was still using the same seal in 1336.[38] A merchant's mark was a geometrical pattern, often formed around a vertical line standing on the shape of an inverted V, a W or a double X and with a 4-shape – right way round or back to front – or a cross or a flag at the top. Rings, crescents

Figs 9, 10, 87

[37] P.R.O. LR 14/1160, 1154.
[38] D.C.D. Misc.4629, 1.4 Spec.6 (Hunter Blair, 54).

88 Anonymous: letter I, early fifteenth century
An initial with crown above, branches at the side, was a design that became increasingly common in the fifteenth century and was often used on signet rings. The letters I (that is, J), R, T and W are often found, suggesting that the letter stood for the owner's forename – but in this example the seal was used in 1424 by Edward Saddler, clerk.

1.1 × 1.0 cm (enlarged).
Public Record Office, E 329/424

and hearts are other frequent elements of the mark and one or two letters may be included. Sometimes there is a shield-shape and occasionally the whole mark is enclosed within a shield, making some patterns difficult to distinguish from a shield of arms. Merchant's marks are often found on the signet rings that became ever more popular in the fourteenth and fifteenth centuries.

But the design that became especially frequent in the fifteenth century, and especially on signet rings, comprised one or two letters, usually in Lombardic form. Two letters would often have a looped cord between them, one letter a crown above with one or more branches at the side. The two letters were presumably the original owner's initials, though the seals were often used by people with quite other names – and these seals must have been made to order. Those with one letter were probably bought ready made and as I, R, T and W are especially common it is likely that the letter usually stood for the purchaser's forename – but this again is no more than an impression. Here, as so often, even the most elementary statistical work on these non-heraldic seals could teach us far more about them than we yet know.

Fig 88

89 Cambridge University, thirteenth century
The earliest known impression of this seal is on a document of 1291, but it was probably made when the university was granted its first charter in 1261. It shows the chancellor, with a book, seated between two scholars in gown and hood; below is bridge over the River Cam.

6.7 × 4.3 cm (actual size).
British Library, Seal lx.10

90 Wardens of the bridge at Rochester, Kent, late fourteenth or early fifteenth century
Many gilds and trusts had a common seal. When the bridge at Rochester was rebuilt in 1397 it was put in the care of wardens, responsible for its upkeep, and the seal probably dates from then or soon after. At one end of the bridge was the chapel of the Trinity, and the Trinity appears on the seal above the bridge itself.

4.8 cm (actual size).
British Museum, Department of Medieval and Later Antiquities, Seal-Die no.187

91 English merchants in the Low Countries, fifteenth century
The legend calls this the seal of English merchants in Flanders, Brabant, Holland and Zeeland. It shows St Thomas of Canterbury above a ship, a design similar to a contemporary English coin, the noble, which shows a ship with the figure of the king rising above it.

4.4 cm (actual size).
British Museum, Department of Medieval and Later Antiquities, Seal-Die no.156

6 SEALS OF CORPORATE BODIES AND THEIR OFFICERS

COMMON SEALS

Even if a personal seal bore its owner's name it might continue in use in other hands after its first owner's death, while an anonymous seal might pass from hand to hand indefinitely. However, no personal seal can have had the longevity intended for a seal made for a supposedly deathless corporate body, ecclesiastical or secular, longevity intended and occasionally achieved – the chapter of Llandaff Cathedral was still using its seal of about 1200 in the mid-sixteenth century and the twelfth-century common seal of the city of Exeter was still in use in the twentieth.[1]

This was not the only peculiarity of corporate seals. We have seen that from the late twelfth century onwards any individual in England might own a seal without question and without presumption – it conferred neither social prestige nor legal status. But for a corporate body to have a common seal implied a claim to legal personality, a claim as an entity to the rights that an individual might have as an owner of property and in a court of law. This was a claim that authority did not lightly admit in medieval Britain. Thus royal grants giving rights to a town, or setting up a gild or a college of chantry priests, would include owning a common seal as one of the privileges of association. Even a formally constituted association might have no common seal: Pembroke College, Cambridge, from its foundation in 1347 had a common seal, which it attached to its original statutes, but in 1311 the scholars of Durham Hall, Oxford, founded in 1249, had to borrow a seal because they had none of their own.[2] Less formal groups were unlikely to have a seal, though on an early-thirteenth-century grant to Margam Abbey in Glamorgan two groups of brothers had each a single seal inscribed 'Sigillum filiorum Wasmihangel' and 'Sigillum filiorum Ruathlan', and in the fifteenth century English merchants in the Netherlands seem to have had a common seal; more typically, the thirteen joint lessees of the market of Ashbourne, Derbyshire, all attached their individual seals to the document of 1286 in which they agreed to respect the borough's customs.[3] When in 1332 the townsmen of St Albans were made to surrender the charter of

Fig 77

Fig 91

[1] D.H. Williams, 'Catalogue of Welsh Ecclesiastical Seals as known down to 1600 A.D. Part III: Capitular Seals', *Archaeologia Cambrensis*, 135 (1986), p.157; H. Lloyd Parry, *The Exeter Civic Seals* (Exeter, 1909), p.1.

[2] W.H. St John Hope, 'Seals of the Colleges and of the University of Cambridge', *Proceedings of the Society of Antiquaries*, 2nd ser. 10 (1883–5), pp.234–5; H. Rashdall, *The Universities of Europe in the Middle Ages*, ed. F.M. Powicke and A.B. Emden (Oxford, 3v., 1936), iii, p.178.

[3] P.R.O. DL 25/891.

privileges they had acquired from the abbey, their common seal had also to be given up and destroyed.[4] Conversely, when a chantry was set up with three chaplains and a warden at Edington, Wiltshire, in 1351, the bishop of Winchester's confirmation forbade them to have a common seal – power was to be vested in the warden alone.[5]

However, permission to have a common seal was often anticipated or simply assumed. The vicars-choral of Lichfield were using one by 1340, though it was not until the late fifteenth century that this was legitimised in their charter.[6] In 1295 villagers at Bromham in Wiltshire were mulcted of £5 – a large sum – by the lord of the manor 'because they made a common seal in contempt of the lord', but as this was ostensibly an agreed fine, not a penal amercement or penalty, it is just possible that they were allowed to keep their seal.[7] Certainly a few village communities had their own seals – Wellow in Nottinghamshire in the thirteenth century,[8] Kingsthorpe in Northamptonshire in the fifteenth – though it is unthinkable that a vill would be accepted as a legal personality and we may wonder what validity its seal could have had in a court of law. More realistically, a number of English boroughs began to use common seals from the early 1190s, apparently in imitation of towns on the Continent and perhaps following the example of London, but without having the right specifically granted, though by the fifteenth century possession of a seal had become one of the tests of an English town's incorporation and thus of its status as a borough.

Fig 92

Before they had a common seal in 1191 the townsmen of Oxford authenticated communal acts with the seal of their gild merchant's alderman, and earlier still, before 1181, with the personal seal of the town reeve.[9] This reflects a general tendency at this period for seals of individual officers to antedate a corporate body's common seal,[10] but the use of the seal of an officer in place of a common seal was not confined to the twelfth century. In 1531 the minoresses of Aldgate, London, sealed a document with 'our Commen seale' – but the seal they attached was the seal of their abbess.[11] In fact when we look at the use of seals by corporate bodies we find less clear distinction than we might expect between the common seal, the seal belonging to a particular office within the organisation, the seal of an officer bearing his or her name and title, and the officer's personal seal without the title of the office. Occasionally the designs of two or more of these seals are linked, as at Inchcolm Abbey, Fife, where the ship with furled sail on the reverse of the common seal recurs on the seal of the abbot, or at Southamp-

[4] J. Tait, *The Medieval English Borough* (Manchester, 1936), p.237.

[5] J.H. Stevenson (ed.), *The Edington Cartulary* (Wiltshire Record Society, vol.42; 1987), p.5.

[6] K. Edwards, *The English Secular Cathedrals in the Middle Ages* (Manchester, 1967), pp.275–6.

[7] G.C. Homans, *English Villagers of the Thirteenth Century* (Cambridge, Mass., 1941), p.332.

[8] ibid., p.336.

[9] Tait, *Medieval English Borough*, pp.231, 235, 239n.

[10] B. Bedos-Rezak, 'Towns and Seals: Representation and Signification in Medieval France', *Bulletin of the John Rylands Library*, 72 (1990), pp.37–8.

[11] P.R.O. LR 14/546.

ton, where a ship with forecastle and sterncastle appears on the common seal of the borough and on successive seals of the office of mayor.

Seal usage by corporate bodies was in fact both complex and diverse. Besides the principal common seal there might be a seal *ad causas*, available to abbot, mayor or other officer for sealing the less important documents – though at St Paul's Cathedral, London, the chapter decided, probably in the thirteenth century, that as this was better known than their principal seal it should be kept and used under the same conditions.[12] Newcastle-upon-Tyne

92 Kingsthorpe, Northamptonshire, fourteenth or fifteenth century
A modern impression from what is probably the only surviving matrix of a village community's common seal. Though a few other villages are known to have had a seal it was a legal anomaly and it is unlikely that a royal court of law would accept the seal as valid. The design, the head of a king, probably refers to the village's name.

3.7 cm (enlarged).
Northamptonshire Record Office, 189p/111

had one in the thirteenth century, but seals *ad causas* were unusual among English and Welsh boroughs, while there are few surviving seals *ad causas* of Scottish corporate bodies, lay or ecclesiastical, earlier than the sixteenth century; however, the burgh of Aberdeen was using one by 1440 and Dunkeld Cathedral chapter by 1502. Glasgow University in 1453 ordered both a common seal and a seal *ad causas* for the rector, but there is some doubt whether the latter was ever made.[13] Much more widespread was the subsidiary common seal often identified in its legend as *secretum*. Pembroke College, Cambridge, sealed its statutes in 1347 not only with its college seal but also with its *secretum* as a counterseal,[14] and this is how a common *secretum* was normally used; an alternative might be to use the seal of an office or an officer's personal seal as a counterseal. Any general pattern in corporate bodies' use of all these various seals has yet to be discerned. It might reflect chronological change, differences between lay and ecclesiastical or between other varieties of organisation, or even regional differences, and it might well throw light on the way their seals were viewed by the corporate bodies

[12] W. Sparrow Simpson (ed.), *Registrum statutorum et consuetudinum ecclesiae cathedralis sancti Pauli Londinensis* (London, 1873), p.132.

[13] G.W. Campbell, 'The Seals of the University of Glasgow', *Transactions of the Glasgow Archaeological Society*, 2nd ser. 4 (1903), pp.65–8.

[14] St John Hope, 'Seals of the Colleges and of the University', pp.234–5.

93 Dean and chapter of Chichester, early thirteenth century
The church building shown on the seal, with 'Templum iusticie' (temple of justice) below, is older than the thirteenth century. That it was copied from an earlier seal and represents the Anglo-Saxon cathedral at Chichester can only be a guess. Several apparently pre-Conquest seals of cathedrals and abbeys show more or less conventional views of church buildings.

6.4 × 8.5 cm (actual size).
British Museum, Department of Medieval and Later Antiquities, Seal-Die no.794

themselves and by the contemporary world at large.

The frequent use of counterseals reflects the preoccupation with security that is another feature of corporate bodies' use of seals. There was a constant fear that a common seal might be used improperly, without full corporate consent, and, to judge from the particular rules that are known to us, devices to guard against this became increasingly elaborate. In 1214 at Salisbury the chapter seal was in the care of two canons; in 1353 it was kept in a chest with three locks, and was to be used only in the presence of all three of the canons who held the keys.[15] In the late thirteenth century the city seal of Winchester was likewise kept in a box with three locks, and the keys were held by two of the mayor's twenty-four counsellors and another citizen, but this box was itself kept in a chest unlocked by two further keys, held by one of the twenty-four and by one other.[16] Matthew Paris tells how in the time of Abbot John de Cella (1195–1214) the common seal at St Albans, left lying among deeds in a chest, was secreted in his sleeve by one of the monks who used it to seal a false and damaging charter; monks of Durham Cathedral reported in 1266 that their former prior, before resigning, had improperly used the common seal to provide for himself from the priory's goods; in 1442–3 the abbot of

[15] Edwards, *English Secular Cathedrals*, pp.207–8.
[16] J.S. Furley, *City Government of Winchester* (Oxford, 1923), pp.53, 174.

Cymmer in Merionethshire petitioned the king because his predecessor, now abbot of Strata Florida, had turned him out of the abbey and was using its seal to make grants and leases of its lands.[17] Certainly stories abound of the misuse not just of common seals but of seals of every kind. But we hear especially of the precautions taken by corporate bodies partly because the rules governing the seals' custody and use are more likely to survive in writing, partly because there was the special risk of internal misuse.

We have seen that important persons' seals might be attached to other persons' documents by way of confirmation. The stability and permanence of any kind of institution made the support of its seal especially attractive and we find the seals of monasteries, cathedral chapters and boroughs, as well as of their officers, all being used for this purpose – always, we may suppose, for a fee. Its seal might thus be not only an expression of a body's authority and legal personality, but also a significant source of profit. In the early fifteenth century the communar of the chapter of Wells accounted for amounts of up to £2.13s.4d. for the use of their seal, apparently in confirming charters of their tenants and others.[18] Sometimes, perhaps often, attaching the common seal or the seal of an officer to someone else's document may have meant that this was registered in the body's records. We find, for instance, private deeds entered in the records of the city of London, and deeds with the mayor's seal attached for 'greater security and testimony'[19] – but whether this registration and confirmatory sealing went together we do not know. The general pattern of usage has never been investigated and could prove of great interest: whose seals were confirmed by which institutions, whether this varied from place to place or in the course of time and how far an element of registration was involved.

But there are many questions unresolved in the use and designs of corporate seals. More work has been done on the seals of monasteries and towns than on the rest, and they are specially discussed here, but much about them remains to be discovered and other groups of which less is known can be of no less interest – the seals of gilds or of non-monastic cathedral chapters, for instance, could well repay systematic study.

Fig 93

MONASTIC SEALS

Fig 3

Besides Edith's seal at Wilton Abbey, seals of six English religious communities are thought to pre-date the Norman Conquest. One, of Durham Cathedral, bears a simple cross; the others all show a building, presumably a conventional view of the church. They come from Canterbury Cathedral

[17] H.T. Riley (ed.), *Gesta abbatum monasterii sancti Albani* (Rolls Series; 3v., 1867–9), i, pp.221–2; W.A. Pantin (ed.), *Documents Illustrating the Activities of the General and Provincial Chapters of the English Black Monks 1215–1540* (Camden 3rd Series; 3v., 1931–7), i, p.245; W. Rees (ed.), *Calendar of Ancient Petitions Relating to Wales* (Board of Celtic Studies, History and Law Series, 28; 1975), p.503.

[18] *Calendar of the Manuscripts of the Dean and Chapter of Wells* (Historical Manuscripts Commission; 2v., 1907–14), ii, pp.27, 34, 48, 52, 58, 64.

[19] E.g. R.R. Sharpe (ed.), *Calendar of Letter-Books of the City of London: Letter-Book D* (London, 1902), p.193; D.C.D. Misc.5574 (Hunter Blair, 824, 3737).

94 Bath Abbey, late eleventh or early twelfth century
The shape, size and design of this seal belong to a late-Anglo-Saxon tradition of monastic seals showing church buildings. They do not seem to have been used to authenticate formal charters until the mid-twelfth century – this impression dates from between 1159 and 1175 – and their original purpose may have been to close letters or to give authority to a messenger.
5.7 cm (actual size).
British Library, Harley Charter 75 A.30

(where the church may have been copied from life), Exeter Cathedral and the abbeys of Athelney, Glastonbury and Sherborne.[20] Few post-Conquest seals of monasteries show simply the building, though Bath and Chertsey Abbeys provide early examples, Holyrood Abbey at Edinburgh and Leeds Priory in Kent rather later ones. More often the building came to be shown with a figure: the abbot within the central arch at Battle, or God the Father and Son above the roof at Scone. Another twelfth-century design that may well have earlier antecedents shows an enthroned figure – St Peter at Gloucester, St Etheldreda at Ely, the abbot at Battle. All these seals are circular, except Holyrood, a pointed oval, but by far the majority of twelfth- and thirteenth-century monastic seals were pointed ovals with the figure of the patron saint of the house – St Guthlac at Crowland in Lincolnshire, St Mary Magdalene at Lanercost in Cumberland, and so on. The earliest examples date from about 1100: oval seals showing St Swithun at Winchester Cathedral Priory and St Peter at Westminster Abbey.[21] The developing cult of the Virgin Mary in the early twelfth century meant that many new monasteries were dedicated to her and thus that she appears on many monastic seals – the first seal of Reading Abbey, founded in 1121, is an early example with Virgin and Child.

Fig 94

Figs 95, 96

Cistercian monasteries, nearly all dedicated to the Virgin Mary, did not follow this pattern.[22] They were first established in England at Waverley in 1128, in Wales at Neath in 1130 and in Scotland at Melrose in 1136, and their seals seem from the start to have been carefully regulated in keeping with the order's austere simplicity and relatively strict discipline. Statutes of the order

[20] T.A. Heslop, 'English Seals from the Mid Ninth Century to 1100', *Journal of the British Archaeological Association*, 133 (1980), pp.7–8.

[21] ibid., pp.13–14.

[22] This account of Cistercian seals is largely based on T.A. Heslop, 'Cistercian Seals in England and Wales', in C. Norton and D. Park (eds), *Cistercian Art and Architecture* (Cambridge, 1983), pp.266–83.

95 St Denys Priory, Hampshire, fourteenth century
The seal shows the martyrdom of St Denys, the priory's patron. On the left is the executioner wielding an axe; on the right is the decapitated saint holding his mitred head in his hands – he was believed to have carried it himself to his place of burial.
4.8 × 2.8 cm (enlarged).
British Library, Seal xliii.34

96 Lanercost Priory, Cumberland, thirteenth century
Many monastic seals of the twelfth and thirteenth centuries were pointed ovals, with the figure of the patron saint of the house. At Lanercost this was St Mary Magdalene, shown holding a palm branch in one hand, the pot of ointment in the other.
7.0 × 4.5 cm (enlarged).
British Library, Seal lxi.35

in 1200 and 1218 reiterate what had probably long been the rule: there should be no common seal, and the abbot might have one seal only, which should show either the abbot himself with his crosier or simply a crosier with a hand grasping it. A modification of 1257 allowed also for a counterseal, with hand and crosier, which was to be specifically so called, *contrasigillum*, in its legend, but which the abbot could also use as a single seal for less important business. All Cistercian seals from Britain in the twelfth and thirteenth centuries conform to these rules; they are small in size, pointed oval in shape, at first of either design but always showing the abbot by the mid-thirteenth century, when the hand and crosier came back for the coun-

Fig 97

97 Dundrennan Abbey, Kirkcudbrightshire, fourteenth Century
This seal is called 'Contra: s'' (*contrasigillum*: counterseal) in the legend and shows a hand grasping a crosier – it thus conforms to the Cistercian statute of 1257 about seals in the order's monasteries. The Cistercian order was exceptional in its detailed rules for the form and design of seals and they do not seem to have been always observed in practice.
3.2 × 2.2 cm (enlarged).
British Library, Seal xlvii.507

98 Knights Templars in England, thirteenth century
The official seals of the Knights Templars usually showed either a building or – as here – the Lamb of God. This seal was used in 1304 by William de la More, the last Grand Preceptor of the English province before the order was finally dissolved in 1312.
3.2 cm (enlarged).
British Library, Harley Charter 83 C.39

terseals. In 1307, to prevent abbots from committing their houses to payments outside the kingdom, the English parliament at Carlisle required all Cistercian monasteries to have a common seal – a change extended to the entire order in 1335 by a papal constitution intended to reduce the abbots' powers in general. At the same time a statute of the order required that the new common seals should be round, with an image of the Virgin, and struck from matrices of brass (*cuprum*). Broadly these injunctions were followed. Cistercian common seals start appearing in England and Wales soon after 1307 – at Grace Dieu in Monmouthshire the abbot's seal was adapted by engraving 'et convent'' on the matrix[23] – and in Scotland in the mid-fourteenth century. But few houses adopted the circular design stipulated in 1335 – only about a quarter of those in England and Wales, and possibly none at all in Scotland. Most Cistercian common seals show the Virgin Mary in a pointed oval and henceforth Cistercian seals could no longer be specially

[23] D.H. Williams, *Catalogue of Seals in the National Museum of Wales* (Cardiff, in progress, 1993–), i, pp.24, 69.

distinguished from those of other monasteries.

Other religious orders seem not to have even tried to regulate seals in this way, though the uniformity of the seals of the military orders, the Hospitallers and Templars, suggests some central direction: a patriarchal cross on the early seals of the Hospitallers' priors and preceptories, the head of John the Baptist on the later ones, and the Lamb of God or a building on those of the Templars. But statutes of Benedictine provincial chapters mention seals only to safeguard their custody and use,[24] and during the thirteenth century the

Fig 98

99 Norwich Cathedral Priory, 1258
This elaborately engraved two-sided seal is dated 1258 in a legend added around the rim from a third matrix. The figure on the front of the seal is identified by the words 'Herbertus fundator' below him – Herbert the founder, that is Bishop Herbert Losinga (1090–1119), in whose time the see was moved from Thetford to Norwich. On the back are the figures of Christ in the rose window and of the Annunciation below.

8.2 cm (reduced).
British Library, Seals lviii.3, 4

common seals of monasteries became generally more varied. To some extent there was a geographical pattern. The seal of St Augustine's Abbey, Canterbury, made in the tenth year of Richard I, 1198–9, and a seal of Westminster Abbey of about the same time started a fashion for two-sided seals, finely and elaborately engraved, with long legends and mostly round, 8 centimetres or more in diameter; these two had enthroned saints on the two sides, but most later examples have on at least one side a fully detailed building with figures. They include the seals of Southwick Priory, Hampshire, and Boxgrove Priory, Sussex (a pointed oval), that were built up from three matrices, and that of Norwich Cathedral Priory which has a legend round the rim

Fig 14
Fig 99

24 Pantin (ed.), *Documents of the English Black Monks*, index under 'seals'.

100 Merton Priory, Surrey, 1241
An outstanding example of the fine and detailed two-sided seals made for some monasteries of south and south-east England from the late twelfth to the fourteenth century, but exceptional in being a pointed oval, not round. On the front are the Virgin and Child, on the back St Augustine; Merton was a priory of Augustinian canons, dedicated to St Mary. The silver matrix was solemnly received there on the eve of the feast of St Lucia, 1241.

8.2 × 5.1 cm (actual size).
British Library, Cotton Charter xxi.25

giving the date 1258. Another with legend round the rim is the much admired mid-thirteenth-century seal of the Augustinian priory at Merton, Surrey, unusual in the group in being a large pointed oval with the Virgin on one side, St Augustine on the other. These seals were made over a period of 150 years for houses of Benedictine monks and Augustinian canons, and even, after 1307, for two Cistercian abbeys, Boxley in Kent and Robertsbridge in Sussex, but they all come from south or south-east England, extending to Norwich in one direction, Glastonbury in the other, with an outlier at Chester. All were probably the work of London goldsmiths. Elsewhere in Britain some monasteries had common seals that were round and two-sided, but rather smaller; most were of simpler workmanship, as at Talley Abbey in Carmarthenshire, but a few were elaborately engraved, as at Arbroath Abbey in Angus, or at Scone Abbey in Perthshire, where the front of the thirteenth- or fourteenth-century seal provides invaluable evidence of the Scottish coronation ceremonies.[25] Some monasteries too, like Bromholm

Fig 100
Fig 22
Fig 109

[25] As shown in an unpublished paper by Professor A.A.M. Duncan.

Priory in Norfolk and Haughmond Abbey in Shropshire, had single-sided round seals. But most religious houses in the fourteenth and fifteenth centuries still had common seals that were pointed ovals with the figure of a saint; many now had a suppliant figure below, and some incorporated shields of arms – the royal arms at Balmerino in Fife, the arms of the Grey family, patrons of the house, at Ruthin in Denbighshire, the arms of the abbey itself at Gloucester, and so on.

Fig 101

101 Dominican Friary at Montrose, Angus, fourteenth century
Like those of bishops and other senior clerics, seals of religious houses in the fourteenth and fifteenth centuries mostly bore the figure of a saint with another figure kneeling below in prayer. The common seal of the Dominicans at Montrose shows the Virgin and Child.
5.3 × 3.5 cm (actual size).
British Library, Seal xlvii.633

This echoes the development of bishops' seals in the thirteenth and fourteenth centuries, when shields of arms were introduced and when the bishop began to be shown only as a suppliant figure below a saint; and we may wonder whether it was monastic seals, which had long borne the figure of a saint, that provided the model – the detailed chronology of these changes has never been explored. Certainly they occur too on the seals of the heads of religious houses, the abbots or priors. For instance, taking two Benedictine priories in south Wales, the late-twelfth-century seal of the prior of Ewenny in Glamorgan shows the prior himself standing holding a book and a scroll, whereas the seal of the prior of Goldcliff in Monmouthshire in 1332 shows the risen Christ and Mary Magdalene, with the prior praying below. But there is another significant difference between them: the Goldcliff seal actually names the prior, William Martel, but the Ewenny seal does not – it is simply the seal of the prior's office.[26] The provision of a seal for each successive holder of the office, to be replaced when it changed hands, was required by the constitutions of the legate Otto in 1237, but seems to have been anticipated in some houses from the late twelfth century. Most abbots and priors appear on their seals in monastic habit, with crosier in the right hand and book in the left, but from the late twelfth century they were often vested as priests and the few mitred abbots are shown in the episcopal vestments they were entitled to wear. What may be the earliest example belonged to

[26] D.H. Williams, 'Catalogue of Welsh Ecclesiastical Seals as known down to 1600 A.D. Part V: Other Monastic Seals', *Archaeologia Cambrensis*, 137 (1988), pp.125–7.

102 Prior of the Dominicans at Glasgow, fourteenth or fifteenth century
This is the seal of the office, not of a particular prior: the holder is not named. It shows a saint – unidentified, but holding a palm branch in one hand, a chalice with perhaps three ears of corn in the other – but without the usual suppliant figure below.
5.1 × 2.9 (enlarged).
British Library, Seal xlvii.548

103 Ralph, abbot of Dunfermline, Fife, c.1275
This seal, in use in 1292, names Ralph in the legend. It shows God the Father, supporting the crucified Christ; the abbot, with crosier, kneels below. He wears a mitre, a privilege granted to the abbey in 1245.
6.0 × 3.5 cm (enlarged).
British Library, Seal xlvii.512

Simon, abbot of St Albans (1167–83), only a few years after the pope had granted the abbey this privilege in 1161. Before named official seals were introduced, some heads of houses used purely personal seals on matters of business. When Samson, abbot of Bury St Edmunds from 1182 to 1211, confiscated thirty-three seals belonging to his monks, permitting only the prior and sacrist to have seals of their own, these were probably mostly personal seals, though the prior's seal that Samson himself used until his own seal was ready must have been an official one.[27] It was most unusual for there to be official seals for any but the head of the house, though they were occasionally to be found in large monasteries – there were seals of office, not naming the holder, for the prior and treasurer of St Augustine's Abbey, Canterbury, in the thirteenth to fifteenth centuries, and for the sacristan and chamberlain of Westminster Abbey in the fifteenth and early sixteenth.

104 London, late twelfth or early thirteenth century
St Paul, with drawn sword, looms above a view of the city and his cathedral church. This is the front of a two-sided seal; on the back is St Thomas of Canterbury, again above a view of London. Though the earliest known reference to the seal is in 1219, it probably dates from the time of London's short-lived recognition as a commune in 1191. The legend, 'Sigillum baronum Londoniarum' (seal of the London barons) reflects the terminology of this time – the 'barons' were London's citizens.
6.7 cm (actual size).
British Library, Seal lxviii.18

TOWN SEALS

Exactly when individual towns first adopted common seals is again a largely unexplored topic, and one of interest not only to sigillography. A very few English boroughs started to use seals in the 1190s, and London was probably among them, though the earliest certain reference to its seal is in 1219.[28] In Scotland, Perth's seal is also mentioned in 1219, but another reference may be as early as the 1190s.[29] It is unclear how far the adoption of a seal might be linked to grants of privileges to a town, in particular grants of the fiscal and attendant administrative rights known as fee-farm or feu-ferme; they certainly went hand in hand at Ipswich in 1200,[30] but in thirteenth-century Scotland Perth, Aberdeen and Elgin all had common seals before feu-ferme was granted.[31] Nor do we know the exact significance, if any, of the differences in wording on early town seals – 'commune sigillum', 'sigillum com-

Fig 104

[27] H.E. Butler (ed.), *The Chronicle of Jocelin of Brakelond* (London, 1949), pp.26, 38.

[28] Tait, *Medieval English Borough*, p.236.

[29] W.C. Dickinson (ed.), *Early Records of the Burgh of Aberdeen* (Scottish History Society, 3rd ser. 49; 1957), pp.xlix–l.

[30] C. Gross, *The Gild Merchant* (Oxford, 2v., 1890), ii, pp.119, 121; the text is discussed by G.H. Martin, *The Early Court Rolls of the Borough of Ipswich* (University College of Leicester, Dept of English Local History, Occasional Papers, 5; 1954), pp.12–14.

[31] Dickinson (ed.), *Early Records of Aberdeen*, pp.xlix–l.

105 Lyme Regis, Dorset, late thirteenth century
Many seaports had a ship on their seal. Here it is shown between on one side Christ crucified, with the Virgin Mary and St John, and on the other St Michael, the town's patron. Flags beside the mast bear the arms of Edward I and his queen, Eleanor of Castile. It was Edward who gave the borough its first charters, in 1284 and 1285, and the seal was probably made then.
5.1 cm (actual size).
British Library, Doubleday Cast F 641

munitatis', 'sigillum burgi', 'sigillum commune burgensium' and others. Private boroughs in England and Wales seem to have been as likely to acquire seals as royal ones; we have seen that Taunton, which belonged to the bishop of Winchester, got a seal at about the same time as Exeter, a royal borough, and the Redvers borough of Christchurch in Hampshire and Trelleck in Monmouthshire, which had a seal with the Clare family arms, were among others that had seals in the thirteenth century. Probably – and in our present state of knowledge we can be no more precise – many, perhaps most, boroughs and other towns in England and Wales had common seals by the end of the thirteenth century, but in Scotland although some burghs already had seals – such as Montrose in Angus and Elgin in Morayshire – they appear widely only in the course of the fourteenth century.

The common seals of towns were nearly all circular, though a very few in England were pointed ovals, such as the thirteenth-century seal of Reading or the late-fourteenth-century seal of Wilton, and in Scotland Rosemarkie in Ross and Cromarty had a pointed-oval seal that may date from the thirteenth century, while Banff in the early fifteenth century was using an oval one. Dunwich in Suffolk was unique in having a seal that was lozenge-shaped. Some towns had large, two-sided, elaborately and finely engraved seals, but these were even more concentrated in south-east England than the similar monastic seals – perhaps town authorities from farther afield were less inclined than monasteries to turn to London goldsmiths instead of local craftsmen. Canterbury, with a seal dated 1318 in a legend on the rim, is an example, and others of the thirteenth and early fourteenth centuries are from Dover and Winchelsea; unlike monasteries, some towns such as Colchester and Rye still had seals made in this style in the fifteenth century. Less elaborate two-sided seals were widely used, as at Inverness, Haverfordwest, York and Kings Lynn, but the majority of town seals were single-sided, offering great variety of size and of fineness of engraving, from Shrewsbury's magnificent seal of 1425, 7.5 centimetres across, with its view of river, bridge, town walls and houses, to the little thirteenth-century seal of Kenfig in Glamorgan, with the design of radiating ears of corn found on many contemporary personal seals.[32]

[32] D.H. Williams, *Welsh History through Seals* (Cardiff, 1982), p.25.

106 Criccieth, Carnarvonshire, late thirteenth century
Though on the coast, Criccieth had on its seal not a ship but the triple-towered gateway more usual for inland towns. On one tower is a griffin, on the other a man – or perhaps a hare – blowing a horn. It is crudely engraved and 'de Crukin' (of Criccieth) appears in the legend as 'ce Drukin'. It probably dates from the creation of the borough in 1284–5.

4.3 cm (actual size).
British Museum, Department of Medieval and Later Antiquities, Seal-Die no.172

107 Bristol, thirteenth or fourteenth century
The two-sided seal of Bristol combines the two most common motifs of municipal seals: the gateway with towers and the ship. On the front the watcher sounds his trumpet, on the back he is perhaps directing the ship into port. Below the ship is a large eel.

7.3 cm (reduced).
British Library, Seals xlv.18, 19

In general, though, there is little correlation between the size of town seals and their design. Two designs predominate: a ship for towns that were ports, and a gateway with three castellated towers for towns that were not. But ship and building might be combined, as at Bristol, and instead of the conventional towered gateway there might be a more or less realistic view of some part of the town – the bridge at Stirling, the church (with ship) at Lydd in Kent, the castle at Rochester – or of the whole town as at Shrewsbury, London and Colchester. We have very few representations of landscape from medieval Britain, and from this point of view these town seals deserve, as a group, closer attention than they have yet received. Coats of arms appear on many town seals, often as the principal element: the arms of the owner of a

Fig 105
Fig 106
Fig 107

108 Inverness, thirteenth or fourteenth century
Many town seals bore coats of arms – of the king, of the town's lord or of the town itself. On the front of the seal of Inverness the Crucifixion is not shown on a shield, but it came to be the burgh's arms. On the back of the seal are the Virgin and Child.
5.4 cm (actual size).
British Library, Seals xlvii.821, 822

private borough, as we have seen at Trelleck, the royal arms in a royal one, as at Appleby in Westmorland, or sometimes in the fifteenth century the arms of the town corporation itself, like the shield with three salmon at Peebles. On the reverse of the two-sided Appleby seal is the martyrdom of St Lawrence; figures of saints in fact occur more often on town seals than coats of arms, and the saint is usually the patron of the local church or monastery. Thus at Dover St Martin dividing his cloak, and at Arbroath the murder of Thomas Becket, appear on the seals of monastery and town alike, and at Glasgow St Kentigern appears on the seals of the burgh, the cathedral chapter and successive bishops. The relationships between these ecclesiastical and town seals – whether one was directly copied from the other – is another topic that deserves to be explored. Other designs include some that are rebuses, playing on the town's name – as the bear on successive seals of Berwick-upon-Tweed, or the two conger eels with a barrel or tun on the fifteenth-century seal of Congleton in Cheshire.[33]

Fig 109

Fig 65

We have seen that at Oxford, town officers were sealing documents for the community before it acquired a common seal; but whether the seals named their office or were simply their personal seals we do not know. An early-thirteenth-century seal bears the name of Adam, gatekeeper of Cardiff, with the picture of a key.[34] In Scotland few, if any, town offices had their own seals. In England, however, town officers – mayors, bailiffs, reeves and others – had seals that named the office but not its holder, reflecting the short

[33] B. Bedos-Rezak discusses the broadly similar designs of French town seals and their iconographic significance in 'Towns and Seals', pp.44–7.

[34] Williams, *Welsh History*, p.25 (from B.L. Harley Charter 75 C.44).

109 Abbey and burgh of Arbroath, Angus, thirteenth century
Sometimes both a town and a local religious house had the same design on their seals. At Arbroath both show the martyrdom of St Thomas of Canterbury; the abbey seal (on the left) was two-sided, with the Virgin and Child on the back; the burgh seal (on the right) single-sided. The burgh seal is known only from the crudely engraved lead matrix – apparently no impressions exist – and its authenticity has been questioned.
Abbey seal 8.1 cm, burgh seal 6.5 cm (actual size).
British Library, Seals xlvii.436, 740

tenure of civic office: it was not worth having a seal engraved that might well be used for no more than a single year.

One group of seals of the mayors of certain English towns calls for particular comment.[35] The Statute of Acton Burnell in 1283 provided that debts could be registered before the mayor, who would issue a recognisance sealed with a special seal supplied by the Crown; the statute names London, York and Bristol, but probably eight further towns were at once brought within its scope. Two years later the Statute of Merchants, among other changes, ordered that the seal should be in two parts, the larger being kept by the mayor, the smaller by the clerk – 'evidently', comments T.F.T. Plucknett, 'there had been some sort of scandal'.[36] By the end of the fourteenth century the number of towns had been increased to at least twenty-five, and from all but four we have either impressions of the seal or the matrix itself. They are of uniform design: the half-length figure of the king, crowned, with a lion on his tunic, and with a castle (at Hull a ship) on each side of his head. The legend reads, variously abbreviated, 'Sigillum Edwardi regis Anglie ad

35 This paragraph is based on C.S. Perceval, 'Seals under the Statute Merchant', *Proceedings of the Society of Antiquaries*, 2nd ser. 7 (1876–8), pp.107–19, and 9 (1881–3), pp.253–6; and W.H. St John Hope, 'Seals of the Statute Merchant', ibid., 2nd ser. 15 (1894–5), pp.435–55.

36 T.F.T. Plucknett, *Legislation of Edward I* (Oxford, 1949), p.140.

recogniciones debitorum apud . . .'; at Oxford the king's name was altered in Richard II's reign, but the seal was still being used without further change in 1457. The seal in two parts meant seal and counterseal, though some seventeenth-century successors were a single seal literally in two pieces, screwed together for sealing.[37] The counterseals are of quite different design and legend from one town to another, and must have been supplied locally; in Exeter at least, the clerk's seal was used independently for quite other purposes.[38] Strictly, of course, these seals for recognisances of debt were not seals of the town itself, but royal seals, for the mayor and clerk were acting as the king's agents.

These seals for recognisances give rise to two general reflections. One stems from their extreme rarity. Whereas nearly half the matrices issued to the mayors survive, we have very few impressions and, indeed, from four places believed to have held them – Hedon, Lostwithiel, Newcastle-upon-Tyne and Worcester – we have neither matrix nor any surviving impression. Yet we might suppose that these seals were much used – but to seal documents that were by their nature ephemeral, unlikely to be kept for long. We should be wary of assuming that surviving matrices and impressions exactly reflect the actual usage of seals in medieval Britain. The other thought is that these seals for recognisances are one of the few groups of seals whose origin and use are well documented. For most we must proceed by inference or surmise and, as we have seen over and over again, research on seals has been spasmodic rather than consistent and has tended to be antiquarian rather than analytical in approach. Innumerable questions remain unanswered, some no more than points of detail, but others with wider historical implications. As T.F. Tout put it in 1920, 'Seals for their own sake may become, and often are, the subjects of the merest antiquarian trifling. Yet there is no reason in the nature of things why seals . . . should not in a humble way be made to contribute their little quota to the great work of reconstituting the past.'[39]

[37] B.L. Additional MS. 43872, f.4 (Newport, Isle of Wight: the division into two parts is clearly visible); Perceval, 'Seals under the Statute Merchant', p.119, and *Proceedings of the Society of Antiquaries*, 2nd ser. 12 (1887–9), pp.408–10 (Carlisle: single part of the seal).

[38] Lloyd Parry, *Exeter Seals*, pp.15 16.

[39] T.F. Tout, *Chapters in the Administrative History of Mediaeval England* (Manchester, 6v., 1920–33), i, p.26.

APPENDIX
LEGENDS ON PERSONAL SEALS

Listed here are legends on medieval British personal seals in the following catalogues and collections, omitting those that simply name the owner:

B C.H. Hunter Blair, 'Durham Seals', parts I–V (personal seals), *Archaeologia Aeliana*, 3rd series 7 (1911), pp.268–360; 8 (1912), pp.46–136; 9 (1913), pp.281–336; 11 (1914), pp.177–277; 12 (1915), pp.287–332

D O.M. Dalton, *Franks Bequest: Catalogue of the Finger Rings* (London, 1912)

DL 25, DL 26 Public Record Office, Duchy of Lancaster Ancient Deeds (Ancient Deeds L, LL)

LR 14, LR 15 Public Record Office, Office of the Auditors of Land Revenue Ancient Deeds (Ancient Deeds E, EE)

O C.C. Oman, *Victoria and Albert Museum, Department of Metalwork: Catalogue of Rings* (London, 1930)

P R.H. Ellis, *Catalogue of Seals in the Public Record Office: Personal Seals*, (London, 2v., 1978–81)

T A.B. Tonnochy, *Catalogue of British Seal-Dies in the British Museum* (London, 1952)

Legends of medieval character on sixteenth-century seals are included. Some of the seals are heraldic, and on these the legend may be a family motto. The list excludes legends on damaged seals where letters lost cannot be supplied with reasonable certainty and also legends that are unintelligible; the printed catalogues explain some that are obscure. Apparently unintelligible legends in the printed catalogues are listed at the end.

Abbreviations have been extended and capital letters, spaces between words and the use of i, j, u and v have been normalised. þ is given as th. Variant spellings are not noted; the entry gives the best version from among the examples listed. A note of the design or the seal-user's name is added where this helps to elucidate the legend, but the figure or symbol of deity or of a saint mentioned in the legend is not specially mentioned.

There is a list of legends in the article on 'Seals' by E. Maunde Thompson in the *Encyclopaedia Britannica* (11th edn, Cambridge, 29v., 1910–11), xxiv, p.542.

a not is gode P1925 (squirrel)
ad Christum pro me sit semper passio Thome P1706
adeu je vole DL 25/2397 (eagle)
agnus dei DL 25/2519
al is fortune DL 25/3530
alak so us T755 (rabbit)
Alano natum fac virgo propiciatum T918
alas e doulc B1046 (stag)
alas haples DL 25/1222
alas je su pris B650, 1297, 1343, 1637, 1756, 2602, 2693; DL 25/33, 853(?), 966(?), 1521, 3441; LR 14/525; P890, 1176, 2040; T748 (hawk taking prey in each case); P2307 (hound taking hare)
alleluia DL 25/3474
alone I ride a river B2523 (hare riding hound)
ama me vere amo te T715
ami amet moun quer avet P386
amie amet B1567; DL 25/2304
amie amet car lel ami avet T730, 731
amor vincit omnia P1370
amore et virtute T348
amur vaint cute rene B184

angelico signo Radulfi carmina gigno (?) B2049
angilus baptista Christi sancta Katerina B447
angnus eat (?) DL 25/756
aquila Johannis B1000, 2577; P1212
archani custos B2265
ardaunt ardaunt T761
atader me comment D509
audi vide tace B1153, 2274
ave D485
ave domina T913
ave domine Jesus Criste P1852
ave gracia plena dominus tecum B1334
ave Maria P527, 1821; T909
ave Maria gracia B597, 823, 2625; DL 25/914, 1361(?), 1730(?), 2236(?), 2584; P77, 230, 1136; T907, 908
ave Maria gracia plena B527, 631, 1175, 1415(?), 1544, 2317, 2476; DL 25/2211, 2254, 2397, 3255; LR 14/501; P365, 658, 1360; T906, 911
ave Maria gracia plena dominus tecum B2078
ave Maria sanctissima ave Katerina P674
ave regina celorum T912

be hit as god wille P943
be war the world B1411
be wel war DL 25/3300; P421
bel velut P1208
benedic nos deus (?) B2409
benedictus deus P224
bi the rode wimen ar wode T762
Billyng' secreta sunt agnus avis cruce leta B240 (Adam of Billingham)
bon amito D513
bon es bon eu bon et (?) P877
brisez vaez lisez craez B2805
bull nott I LR 14/496 (ox's head; John Bowes)

ca le tirout T747 (hawk taking rabbit)
caperas patior hec reus esse reor B1294
caput Johannet P431
caput Johannis DL 25/3346
caput Johannis in disco B173, 449, 579, 2378
caput nazarei sigillum B1286
caput servi dei B1300, 1780; T933 (man's head in each case); B2174 (stag's head)
caput servi veri dei P781 (man's head)
cela segreta Willelmi P956 (William son of William of Ashford)
Christi concipiens clave ve quia tollis ave T915
clausa secreta tego T705
conserva Ricardum Nicholas tuum DL 25/1861
crede capud B2728 (man's head)
crede ferenti B1523; DL 25/1657, 2180(?), 3423; T709, 710
crede flori sicut ori DL 25/2252 (cross flory between flowers)
crede michi B392, 1709, 2967; DL 25/194, 832, 841, 1881, 2072, 2274, 2894, 3238, 3441, 3573; P2306; T711, 712, 713, 714
crede michi et est satis T931
crede Petri servo (?) DL 25/1262, 2008
credite patribus LR 14/85
credo deo salutis (?) B1987
crux precibus Thome cruce de Thomam rege tu me P1258 (Thomas Cross)
crux sancta dei B902
cu mieux P1959 (duck)
cur spinas Phebo gero te Waltere docebo P348 (moon and man with bundle of sticks; Walter of Grendon)

dat deus omne bonum T932
de fin quer voli aver P1286
de Lancastre martir voudroi priez dieu pur moi (?) P154
de li pensez par ky me avez DL 25/158; P920
de par dieux P110
deo gras B866, 2053
deum time B2828; DL 25/2074
deus caritas est DL 25/1964
deus reus DL 25/1557, 1875(?)
diu vivatis LR 14/707
dives durus B718
do for me and I for the (?) DL 25/2173
dominus Jesus DL 25/842
dred P1386

ecce agnus DL 25/3441; T903
ecce agnus dei B21, 194, 207, 2267; DL 25/1016, 1234, 1310, 1345, 1775, 1934, 2403, 3441, 3576; LR 14/892/18, 1155, 1176; P438, 709, 932, 1395; T901, 902, 904
ecce agnus dei Johannes est nomen B532
ecce agnus domini DL 25/980
ecce agnus sine macula P779
ecce angnus dei ave Meria T900
ecce Jovis DL 25/3579 (eagle)
Edmundi Thome prece matris child loke to me T929
ego secreta tego D226
eis mitis mira miseris miserere Maria B1118
Emanuel B1154
emeut le mu P875
en cest B787
en honi espoyer P199

en lel amour su assis B1165 (rabbit sitting)
envie B1654
esperance B1959, 1968, 1968a
est Ade signum vir femina vipera lignum T930 (Adam, Eve, serpent and tree)
est avis ascendens T746 (eagle)
esto fidelis DL 25/2168, 3628
esto prudens et serpens B2985
exultate deo flos caput atque leo P331 (man's head and lion)

fahcun gentil B999 (hawk taking rabbit)
fei me tent DL 25/1724
fiat fiat amen B1327
foy pour devoir P712
foy rivolde P517
frange lege lecta tege T706
frange lege tege B552, 575, 1005, 1578, 2183, 2435, 3003; DL 25/391, 1713, 1945, 2073, 2315, 2462, 2419, 2916(?), 3109, 3190, 3420; LR 14/560; P1309, 1385; T359
frange scienda tege DL 25/2345
frater T de B que pando dulciam pro me T562 (Thomas of Bredon?)
fraxine sub fronde Rogeri carmina conde B917 (Roger of Esh)
frugis apis vitis cras pocula trina sititis P180 (three heads joined)

gauther hanlok B571
go Gille to ete thi fille P1427 (mare suckling foal)
go to God Gatishevid B1057 (Adam of Gateshead)
God help T935
God help that best may P144
God help the pope B1542
greet moy en bone foy B744
grene ginger P344 (John Green)
gret wel Gibbe oure cat P756 (cat and mouse; Gilbert Stone)

hac duplici formaque signatur tibi forma B2706 (design divided in two)
hasard thin hod is min DL 25/1684 (dog and hare gaming)
hayl ape hayl B994 (ape)
he who best may P1359
hec est aquila B1194 (eagle)
helpe moder of mercy B711, 1117
Henrici [...]ton signum flos avis leo lignum (?) B2173 (flower, bird, lion and tree)
her DL 25/1515
her is none bot a fische and har P1397 (hare and fish; Thomas of Fishburn)
heyl ape ylu T758 (ape)
heyl heyl heyl B2036 (ape)
hoc est sigillum si is salva Jerusillum (?) B1458
hoc signum pro me Thoma dat passio Thome B1909 (Thomas de Nova Haya)
holy my servise P263
hot ary he hot (?) B2439 (fish cooking)
houl ape P949 (ape and owl)
Hugonis Tesdal clavis mater et agnus avis (?) B2398 (Virgin and Child, Lamb of God and bird; Hugh of Teesdale)

I byde grace P3
I crake notis B39, 2462; DL 25/1349, 3350(?) (squirrel in each case)
I crake notis her B203
I knak nots T754 (squirrel)
I mene wel DL 26/54; P657
I notis crak on lyoun bak B1640 (squirrel and sleeping lion)
I ride P869 (hare riding hound)
I ride alone a revere B1121 (hare riding hound)
icesto sel bel est de amour lel B582, 763(?), 808(?)
ici dort le lioun fort B114, 830, 890, 1088, 1375
ici gist Corbin le bon B2241 (sleeping dog)
ignota noto T765
in all DL 25/1139
in amore DL 25/666
in cruce amor meus (?) B2166
in domino confido P145
in ea Sancta Caterina T928
in principio P1310
in principio erat verbum B2787
inmutabile signum T766
inventio crucis ostendit gaudia lucis (?) B2394
is sit salva bonis Willelmi vita patronis B1135 (William of Gretton)

jagre su de grac et vertu DL 25/3241
je cheytys suy en sel nis P343
je espoyr B1966
je su criue P2075
je su leel P1403; T724
je su quer leal P2
je su rey de beites T742 (lion)
je su sel a Thomas Viel P827 (Thomas Viel)
je su sel bon e lel B1222; P277(?); T723
je su sel de amour lel B174, 360, 1603, 1972(?), 2124, 2208, 2426; DL 25/1919; P1629; T718, 721
je su sel de tous pars lel B2494
je su sel jolis e gai e lel T722

milito pugno tego B2958, 2959
mitis sim apostolorum B362
mive si vis DL25/1563, no.1
mon bien mon dam P1581
mon dezir P2312
mon quer aiez en garde (?) B175
mon quer avez nel deceve T733
monte sepulta sina pro Thoma sis Katerina P1436 (Thomas of Garton)
mor no lesse bot ape oule asse B1478 (ape holding owl and riding ass)
moun quer vous bayle P2154
mun cuer avet T734
munio secreta B1790

nazarenus rex judeorum B1957
ni le doyt eie croit bene seit B572
nicol P181
non other P1328
now ys thus D536
nowel D306
nunquam vitabis culpam si multa loqueris T707

o bone Jesu esto michi Jesus P1751
oculi mei semper ad dominum T911
offrance B1670
ora pro me pia Katarina P488
ora pro nobis amice Christi Johannes (?) DL 25/1519
ora pro oy sancte Andre B22
oritur celus LR 14/501
osanna LR 15/8
owe best P2314

par ces seignours attendrei honours B918 (four shields of arms)
parce Jesu queso peccati wlnere leso B1053, 1055
passione trina tua salva licet Katerina (?) DL 25/1615
pastor meas dele culpas B1635, 2389
penset de lipard isuci B2198(?), 2353 (sleeping lion in each case); B2267(?) (sleeping dog and lion's heads); DL 25/1575 (lion on shield of arms)
pensez de bien fere T763
perceto testimonium de vero (?) P407
Peter and Pawil prai for mi sawl B2718
plentee P452
poi vaut vivre sans lel ami T737
por grac DL 25/1184
posco Cuthberte Christo vivente B1604
prece Laurenti peccamina in se petenti P471
prius DL 25/719
prive sel DL 25/1266(?), 1681; P330
prive soit P260
prive su B1103, 1369; DL 25/541, 1514, 2304, 3101; T696, 697
prive su e pou conu B2213(?), 2308; T700, 701
prive su ea T699
prive su pru T698
pro signo certi tu scripto crede Roberti DL 25/1959; P2288
pur luttru P1107
pur moy D290

quanta ago quanta rego pietatem reformo P1326
que tibi lego lege T704
qui ligat ic solvit Petrus celoque remittit T921
qui me porte siest le mus T760
quia inde LR 15/8

Radulphi memores sitis Maria Johannes LR 14/527 (Ralph of Windsor)
recobo T361
respice tecta ec perfice lecta tege (?) B1507
Rogerus quasi rosam gerens T618
ryswyc P986

sainte Caterine prie pur moy P515
salve crux santa DL 25/2189
salve regina misericordie P545, 693
salvi hi iconomi sitis Maria Johannes LR 14/1152
sancta Katerina B272; P665; T927
sancta Katerina ora pro me B2506; P229
sancta Margareta ora pro me P253
sancta Maria Magdalena B140
sancta Maria regina celi (?) B1898
sanctus Laurencius DL 25/1910, 1911, 3447
sanctus Petrus B2397
sanctus Thomas cantuariensis P368
santa Maudel DL 25/1561
Sarra est nomen eius DL 25/3389 (Sarah widow of Gilbert of Tuddenham)
saunca Caterina T926
sauncte Laurenti P2039
sauncte Petri ora T923, 924
say the beste LR 14/488
scutum Ricardi conservent tres leopardi P1325 (three lion's heads and shield of arms; Richard of Eccleshall)
secreti mei DL 25/3288
secreti signum Johannis piscis avis leo T759 (fish, bird and lion)
secretum meum DL 25/1411
seel deguse su apele B905, 2686(?)
sel mercy P1557
si non vis juveni credere crede seni P1903 (double-

The following incomplete or apparently unintelligible legends in the printed catalogues are listed without word divisions or normalisation of letter forms.

aliva. . .emvnqvera B1824
amameetegotecra T716
amiisave B1404
anisvnesvdev B1322
avemead T910

capvdnostrvm. . .B2499
. . .cristicenacristikarissim. . .B1628
crvotgrais P1809

dangenriencis B1744
darogocvthberte. . .ilihvivsreaerte B1335
droith'abon B1254

ecceagnvsdeigv B831
engrace. B2615
enhienvvlt B2056
exornatthomesigilv.p.rsiot B1570

frange. . .legesecreta B570
frvs. . . .eseitho.iefrvssamieseithonie B1527

gentoleovnaciesihvn P232

heyladekheta T757
hn. . . .etloyall B2486
hostisedererbilatorest B1262
hovanitatisimilfse B1235

idadsecci T905
iesvsele..lel B2024
ievovsdvovs B2281
imiacvsanisnostratsert.. B1388
interiorategosi. . . . . . .clavsarev. . .B1994
iomeciovme B884
iovcoov. . .B1470

katerinevenrohymhyne P1698

lecoas P1695

lesvssigneprivea.elvvc. . . . . .nde B2122
loiatirodsini B1595
lovemea. B1287
lovemeandis'ev' B2708

mita B2028
mvndvmcreavinedg P1449

natimotacvpeddeipvsneydevesanere B702

orare. . . . . . .virgomaria B2407
oroiohannivlvndamdaparadisvm T925

passandhntevatcnctte P1488
pelicansdicor. . .pvll.crvc. . .B2717
permalarexmie. . .ricovirgoivv. . . .B2293
privesmiv B2573
privesoivdi P79
priviesividv P1666

respicetectaleg. B1119
revavrmei T767
rsavlvai P731

s'.fertpvermr.petrvshicestmvtaqfr B1503
sdixpadive P587
seelicimodendina. . .B822
seo.tcvsle B2395
sinvr D288
siprdive P847
sistequsnictas. B2094
s'tispvrmoyilvsairi B786

tvtsisanniscuhtiskaterinaiohannis B2149

wareme. . .et B1011
weleadvisbebit P2316/3

SELECT BIBLIOGRAPHY

CATALOGUES

The only catalogues that cover all known seals of particular classes are J.H. Stevenson and M. Wood, *Scottish Heraldic Seals: Royal, Official, Ecclesiastical, Collegiate, Burghal, Personal* (privately printed, 3v., 1940), which describes all medieval seals from Scotland except non-heraldic personal seals but without illustrations, and D.H. Williams, 'Catalogue of Welsh Ecclesiastical Seals as known down to 1600 A.D.', in six parts in *Archaeologia Cambrensis*, vols 133–8 (1984–9), which includes monastic seals and personal seals with religious devices and which is well illustrated.

Of catalogues of particular collections of seal impressions by far the largest is W.de G. Birch, *Catalogue of Seals in the Department of Manuscripts in the British Museum* (London, British Museum, 6v., 1887–1900), which covers detached seals and casts as well as those on documents, English and Welsh in vols 1–3, Scottish in vol. 4; it includes non-heraldic personal seals only for Scotland and has few illustrations. R.C. Fowler, 'Seals in the Public Record Office', *Archaeologia*, 74 (1925), pp.103–16, pl.XXXI–XXXV, lists and illustrates seventy seals of particular interest. R.H. Ellis, *Catalogue of Seals in the Public Record Office* (London, H.M. Stationery Office, 3v., 1978–86), represents the start of what has been planned as a full catalogue with a separate series of volumes for each category of seal; those that have appeared are two volumes of personal seals (from the 'S' classes of Ancient Deeds) and one of monastic, and over a third of the seals are illustrated. Only the first volume has so far appeared of D.H. Williams, *Catalogue of Seals in the National Museum of Wales* (Cardiff, National Museum of Wales, 1993); it covers matrices as well as Welsh seal impressions and papal bullae, all fully illustrated. The substantial catalogues of his own collection of casts by H. Laing, *Descriptive Catalogue of Impressions from Ancient Scottish Seals* (Bannatyne Club, vol.91, and Maitland Club, vol.68; 1850) and *Supplemental Descriptive Catalogue of Ancient Scottish Seals* (Edinburgh, Edmonston and Douglas, 1866), are effectively superseded by the catalogues of Birch and of Stevenson and Wood (above). There are many British seals in the great collections of casts in the Archives Nationales in Paris, listed in M. Douët d'Arcq, *Ministère d'État: Archives de l'Empire. Collection de Sceaux* (Paris, Henri Plon, 3v., 1863–8), and G. Demay, *Inventaire des Sceaux de la Collection Clairambault* (Paris, Imprimerie Nationale, 2v., 1885–6).

Outside national collections, C. Hunter Blair, 'Durham Seals', in nine parts in *Archaeologia Aeliana*, 3rd ser., vols 7–9 (1911–13), 11–16 (1914–19), is a well-illustrated catalogue (taking as its starting-point the lists of W. Greenwell) of the seals in the muniments of the Dean and Chapter of Durham, outstanding in their number – 3755 are listed – the early dates of some and the proportion of Scottish seals. Other catalogues of particular archives and repositories in Britain include T.D. Tremlett and P.D. Walne, 'A Catalogue of some Medieval Armorial Seals in the Berkshire Record Office', *Berkshire Archaeological Journal*, 55 (1956), pp.32–47, F.C. Morgan and P.E. Morgan, *A Concise List of Seals belonging to the Dean and Chapter of Hereford Cathedral* (Woolhope Naturalists' Field Club, 1966), and D. Reid of Robertland and A. Ross, *A Catalogue of Seals in the University of Glasgow* (Oxford, Oxford Microform Publications, 1975). The only substantial regional catalogue is C.H. Hunter Blair, 'Seals of Northumberland and Durham', *Archaeologia Aeliana*, 3rd ser. 20, pp.69–186; 21, pp.38–120b, which excludes those listed in his 'Durham Seals' (above) but still covers over 1000 seals; F. Taylor, 'Selected Cheshire Seals (12th–17th Century) from the Collections in the John Rylands Library', *Bulletin of the John Rylands Library*, 26 (1941–2), pp.393–412, describes only twenty seals.

The most substantial catalogue of matrices is A.B. Tonnochy, *Catalogue of British Seal-Dies in the British Museum* (London, British Museum, 1952), which includes a valuable introduction and many illustrations of modern impressions. P.H. Nelson, 'Some British Medieval Seal-Dies', *Archaeological Journal*, 93 (1936), pp.13–44, pl.I–IV, is a detailed catalogue of his own collection of one hundred matrices, with illustrations of nearly half. Early dies are described, with full bibliographies, in E. Okasha, *Hand-List of Anglo-Saxon Non-Runic Inscriptions* (Cambridge, University Press, 1971), pp.71, 107–8, 118–20. Medieval signet rings are listed, and a few illustrated, in O.M. Dalton, *Franks Bequest: Catalogue of the Finger Rings* (London, British Museum, 1912), pp.xxix–xxxii, 37–98, and C.C. Oman, *Victoria and Albert Museum, Department of Metalwork: Catalogue of Rings* (London, Board of Education, 1930), pp.8–16, 85–101.

GENERAL WORKS AND BIBLIOGRAPHIES

The best up-to-date short introduction to sigillography is M. Pastoureau, *Les Sceaux* (Typologie des Sources du Moyen Âge Occidental, no.36; Turnhout, Brepols, 1981), but there are also good brief guides in English: H.S. Kingsford, *Seals* (Helps for Students of History, no.30; London, Society for Promoting Christian Knowledge, 1920); C.H. Hunter Blair, 'A Note upon Mediaeval Seals with Special Reference to those in Durham Treasury', *Archaeologia Aeliana*, 3rd ser. 17 (1920), pp.244–313, pl.I–VIII, in effect an introduction to his 'Durham Seals' (above); and [H. Jenkinson], *Guide to Seals in the Public Record Office* (London, H.M. Stationery Office, 1954; 2nd edn 1968) which, though focused on the Public Record Office, is the fullest account (it is an expanded version of his 'The Study of English Seals: Illustrated chiefly from Examples in the Public Record Office', *Journal of the British Archaeological Association*, 3rd ser. 1 (1937), pp.93–127). Two encyclopaedia articles are also of particular interest: E. Maunde Thompson, 'Seals', in *Encyclopaedia Britannica* (11th edn, Cambridge, University Press, 29v., 1910–11), xxiv, pp.539–43, and B. Bedos-Rezak, 'Seals and Sigillography, Western European', in J.R. Strayer (ed.), *Dictionary of the Middle Ages* (New York, Charles Scribner's Sons, 13v., 1982–9), xi, pp.123–31. Longer general works are more descriptive than analytical in approach: W.de G. Birch, *History of Scottish Seals from the Eleventh to the Seventeenth Century* (Stirling, Eneas Mackay, 2v., 1905–7), which covers royal seals in volume 1, ecclesiastical and monastic seals in volume 2; J.H. Bloom, *English Seals* (London, Methuen, 1906); and W.de G. Birch, *Seals* (London, Methuen, 1907), which includes foreign seals as well as British. B. Bedos-Rezak, 'Medieval Seals and the Structure of Chivalric Society', in H. Chickering and T.H. Seiler (eds), *The Study of Chivalry: Resources and Approaches* (Kalamazoo, Medieval Institute Publications, Western Michigan University, 1988), pp.313–72, looking at western Europe in general, shows how seal designs illustrate the social structure and social concepts of the Middle Ages, while on a smaller canvas D.H. Williams, *Welsh History through Seals* (Cardiff, National Museum of Wales, 1982), is an interesting introduction to the way seals reflect historical development. Though concerned mostly with French seals, many of the essays by B. Bedos-Rezak reprinted in her *Form and Order in Medieval France: Studies in Social and Quantitative Sigillography* (Aldershot, Variorum, 1993) are relevant to Britain; they include articles mentioned individually below.

M.T. Clanchy, *From Memory to Written Record: England 1066–1307* (2nd edn, Oxford, Blackwell, 1993), places seals in the context of the development of written records. Contributions by T.A. Heslop to the well-illustrated catalogues of two important exhibitions discuss the manufacture, design and use of seals in England down to the fifteenth century: G. Zarnecki, J. Holt and T. Holland (eds), *English Romanesque Art 1066–1200* (London, Arts Council of Great Britain, 1984), pp.298–319, and J. Alexander and P. Binski (eds), *Age of Chivalry: Art in Plantagenet England 1200–1400* (Royal Academy, London, 1987), pp.114–17 and nos 94–7, 141–4, 193–201, 275–86, 453–62, 670–7. Two designs that occur on various categories of British and other seals, castles and ships, are discussed by J. Cherry, 'Imago Castelli: the Depiction of Castles on Medieval Seals', *Château Gaillard: Études de castellologie médiévale*, 15 (1992), pp.83–90, and by H.H. Brindley, 'Medieval Ships', in twelve parts in *The Mariner's Mirror*, 1–4 (1911–14), who discusses the details of ships shown on seals and elsewhere. H.S. Kingsford, 'The Epigraphy of Medieval English Seals', *Archaeologia*, 79 (1929), pp.149–78, is a painstaking analysis of the letter-forms in seal legends, with many examples of each letter in turn.

Though bibliographies of works on seals are in preparation for the International Council on Archives, those published are guides only to the older literature: [R.H.S. Smith], *A List of Books and Pamphlets in the National Art Library, South Kensington Museum, illustrating Seals* (London, H.M. Stationery Office, 1886), pp.13–27, and S.T. Cope, 'Heraldry, Flags and Seals: a Select Bibliography, with Annotations, covering the

Period 1920 to 1945', *The Journal of Documentation*, 4 (1948), pp.92–146 (issued also as a pamphlet). *Conseil International des Archives, Comité de Sigillographie: Vocabulaire international de la sigillographie* (Pubblicazioni degli Archivi di Stato, Sussidi no.3; Rome, Ministerio per i Beni Culturali e Ambientali, 1990), defines the terms used – in twelve languages – in describing seals.

MATRICES

For catalogues of matrices see above. S.E. Rigold, 'Two Common Species of Medieval Seal-Matrix', *Antiquaries Journal*, lvii (1977), pp.324–9, discusses matrices that are flat-backed or ridged, and those engraved at the base of an hexagonal pyramid. F. Madden, 'Remarks on the Matrix of the Seal of Boxgrave Priory, in Sussex', *Archaeologia*, 27 (1838), pp.375–80, describes how the multiple-matrix seal was used, and another peculiar type of matrix is discussed by H.S. Kingsford, 'Seal Matrices with Screw-out Centres', *Antiquaries Journal*, 4 (1924), pp.249–56.

Two important articles discuss who made the matrices and how: H.S. Kingsford, 'Some English Medieval Seal-Engravers', *Archaeological Journal*, 97 (1940), pp.155–80, and T.A. Heslop, 'Seals as Evidence for Metalworking in England in the Later Twelfth Century', in S. Macready and F.H Thompson (eds), *Art and Patronage in the English Romanesque* (Occasional Paper, new ser. 8; London, Society of Antiquaries, 1986), pp.50–60. J. Blair and N. Ramsay (eds), *English Medieval Industries: Craftsmen, Techniques, Produce*, (London, Hambledon Press, 1991), especially pp.119–20, 148–50, 159, describe seal-making in the general context of medieval English crafts.

WAX

The wax in medieval seals is discussed by J.J. Dobbie and J.J. Fox, 'The Composition of some Mediaeval Wax Seals', *Journal of the Chemical Society*, 105 (1914), pp.795–800, and by C. Woods, 'The Nature and Treatment of Wax and Shellac Seals', *Journal of the Society of Archivists*, 15 (1994), pp.203–14.

SEAL BAGS

G. Robinson and H. Urquhart, 'Seal Bags in the Treasury of the Cathedral Church of Canterbury', *Archaeologia*, 84 (1934), pp.163–211, describe in detail this unique collection, with reference to other seal-bags surviving in England.

SEALS BEFORE 1100

The early use of seals in England is described in two important articles: P. Chaplais, 'The Anglo-Saxon Chancery: from the Diploma to the Writ', *Journal of the Society of Archivists*, 3, no.4 (1966), pp.160–76 (reprinted in F. Ranger (ed.), *Prisca Munimenta: Studies in Archival and Administrative History presented to Dr A.E.J. Hollaender* (London, University of London Press, 1973), pp.43–62), and T.A. Heslop, 'English Seals from the Mid Ninth Century to 1100', *Journal of the British Archaeological Association*, 133 (1980), pp.1–16. The earliest royal seals are all listed, illustrated and discussed by T.A.M. Bishop and P. Chaplais (eds), *Facsimiles of English Royal Writs to A.D. 1100* (Oxford, Clarendon Press, 1957), pp.xix–xxiv. Another article by T.A. Heslop, 'Twelfth-Century Forgeries as Evidence for Earlier Seals: the Case of St Dunstan', in N. Ramsay, M. Sparks and T. Tatton-Brown (eds), *St Dunstan: his Life, Times and Cult* (Woodbridge, Boydell Press, 1992), pp.299–310, uses an interesting approach to the form of now-lost early seals.

ROYAL SEALS

On the hierarchy of royal seals in England, how it developed and how the seals were used, crucial works are T.F. Tout, *Chapters in the Administrative History of Mediaeval England: the Wardrobe, the Chamber and the Small Seals* (Manchester, University Press, 6v., 1920–33), H.C. Maxwell-Lyte, *Historical Notes on the Use of the Great Seal of England* (London, H.M. Stationery Office, 1926), and P. Chaplais, *English Royal Documents, King John – Henry VI* (Oxford, Clarendon Press, 1971). On the great seals, A.B. Wyon and A. Wyon, *The Great Seals of England* (London, Eliot Stock, 1887), is a definitive book, giving for each successive seal a full description, illustrations and a list of impressions, but subsequent work has shown the need for substantial correction: H. Jenkinson, 'The Great Seal of England: Some Notes and Suggestions', *Antiquaries Journal*, 16 (1936), pp.8–28 (on fifteenth-century seals and on duplicate seals for the king's absences abroad); H. Jenkinson, 'A New Seal of Henry V', *Antiquaries Journal*, 18 (1938), pp.382–90; Bishop and Chaplais (eds), *Facsimiles of English Royal Writs*, pp.xix–xxiv (above, on the seals of Edward the Confessor and William I); P. Chaplais, 'The Seals and Original Charters of Henry I', *English Historical Review*, 75 (1960), pp.260–75 (reprinted in his *Essays in Medieval Diplomacy and Administration* (London, Hambledon Press, 1981)); P. Chaplais, *Piers Gaveston: Edward II's Adoptive Brother* (Oxford, Clarendon Press, 1994), pp.37–41 (on duplicate seals for the king's absences abroad). B. Wilkinson, 'The Seals of the Two Benches under Edward III', *English Historical Review*, 42 (1927), pp.397–401, and H. Jenkinson, 'A Seal of Edward II for Scottish Affairs', *Antiquaries Journal*, 11 (1931), pp.229–39, deal with particular deputed seals, and deputed seals as a group are discussed at length by H. Jenkinson, 'The Great Seal of England: Deputed or Departmental Seals', *Archaeologia*, 85 (1936), pp.293–340. H. Jenkinson, 'The Great Seal of England', *Journal of the Royal Society of Arts*, 101 (1952–3), pp.550–63, is a brief survey of great and deputed seals, while their symbolism as icons of royal power is discussed by B. Bedos-Rezak, 'The King Enthroned, a New Theme in Anglo-Saxon Royal Iconography: the Seal of Edward the Confessor and its Political Implications', in J. Rosenthal (ed.), *Kings and Kingship* (Binghamton, Center for Medieval and Early Renaissance Studies, 1986), pp.53–88 (reprinted in her *Form and Order*, above), and J. Steane, *The Archaeology of the Medieval English Monarchy* (London, Batsford, 1993), pp.22–30. Articles on particular royal signets are W.S. Walford and A. Way, 'Examples of Mediaeval Seals', *Archaeological Journal*, 18 (1861), pp.49–55 (on the signet of the eagle), and P.E. Lasko, 'The Signet Ring of King Richard I of England', *Journal of the Society of Archivists*, 1, no.8 (1963), pp.333–5.

Much less has been written on the royal seals of medieval Scotland. A. Wyon, 'The Great Seals of Scotland', *Journal of the British Archaeological Association*, 45 (1889), pp.95–111, 235–49, is slight, but R.K. Hannay, 'The Early History of the Scottish Signet', in *The Society of Writers to His Majesty's Signet* (Edinburgh, Society of Writers to the Signet, 1936), pp.3–51, is a full account of the lesser seals from the first appearance of the signet in the mid-fourteenth century, to which W.C. Dickinson, '"Our Signet of the Unicorn"', *Scottish Historical Review*, 26 (1947), pp.147–8, adds a note. A.A.M. Duncan (ed.), *The Acts of Robert I, King of Scots 1306–1329* (Regesta Regum Scottorum, vol.5; Edinburgh, University Press, 1988), pp.178–97, is a detailed account of seals and sealing at the time when the privy seal first came into regular use, and G.G. Simpson, 'Kingship in Miniature: a Seal of Minority of Alexander III, 1249–1257', in A. Grant and K.J. Stringer (eds), *Medieval Scotland: Crown, Lordship and Community: Essays presented to G.W.S. Barrow* (Edinburgh, Edinburgh University Press, 1993), pp.131–9, identifies the apparently unique seal made for a king who was a minor.

ARISTOCRATIC AND HERALDIC SEALS

These seals are especially well – or even exclusively – covered by most of the catalogues listed above. The best general guide to English upper-class seals is C.H. Hunter Blair, 'Armorials upon English Seals from the Twelfth to the Sixteenth Centuries', *Archaeologia*, 89 (1943), pp.1–26, which discusses the origins and development of heraldry on equestrian and armorial seals, with over 200 illustrations. M.P. Siddons, 'Welsh Equestrian Seals', *National Library of Wales Journal*, 23 (1983–4), pp.292–318, is a valuable illustrated list of extant impressions. W.R. MacDonald, *Scottish Armorial Seals* (Edinburgh, William Green and Sons, 1904), is a compilation chiefly of late-medieval seals. The most thorough study of one particular earldom's seals is T.A. Heslop, 'The Seals of the Twelfth-Century Earls of Chester, *Journal of the Chester Archaeological Society*, 71 (1991), pp.179–97, which examines in detail not only the earls' principal seals but their gems and counterseals as well. G. Henderson, 'Romance and Politics on some Medieval English Seals', *Art History*, 1 (1978), pp.26–42, discusses the iconographic and other significance of gems set as signets, seals showing a man fighting a beast and other seals of the Quincy and FitzWalter families. J.R. Studd, 'The Seals of the Lord Edward', *Antiquaries Journal*, 58 (1978), pp.310–19, shows what seals were used by the future Edward I and

Lord Howard de Walden, *Some Feudal Lords and their Seals MCCCJ* (privately printed, 1904), describes and illustrates the fine range of heraldic seals on the Barons' Letter.

Recently the heraldic seal has come to be of interest to social historians, particularly in the definition of the nobility and the diffusion of coats of arms to lower social ranks. This was discussed for France by P. Adam-Even, 'Les sceaux d'écuyers au XIIIe siecle', *Archives héraldiques suisses*, 66 (1951), pp.19–29, and by B. Bedos-Rezak, 'The Social Implications of the Art of Chivalry', in E.R. Haymes (ed.), *The Medieval Court in Europe* (Houston German Studies 6; Munich, 1986), pp.142–75 (reprinted in her *Form and Order*, above); and for Britain by D. Crouch, *The Image of the Aristocracy in Britain, 1000–1300* (London, Routledge, 1992), especially pp.226–8, 232–7, 242–6. The use of heraldic seals by knights and esquires is examined in two works by P.R. Coss, *The Knight in Medieval England 1000–1400* (Stroud, Sutton Publishers, 1993), pp.79–81, and, more particularly, 'Knights, Esquires and the Origins of Social Gradation in England', *Transactions of the Royal Historical Society*, 6th ser. 5 (1995).

WOMEN'S SEALS

Little has been written on women's seals. C.H. Hunter Blair, 'Armorials upon English Seals' (above) includes a section on women's heraldic seals (pp.19–26), and the systematic analysis of the seals of French women, noble and non-noble, in two articles by B. Bedos-Rezak is relevant to Britain: 'Women, Seals and Power in Medieval France, 1150–1350', in M. Erler and M. Kowaleski (eds), *Women and Power in the Middle Ages* (Athens, University of Georgia Press, 1988), pp.61–82, and 'Medieval Women in French Sigillographic Sources', in J.T. Rosenthal (ed.), *Women and Sources of Medieval History* (Athens, University of Georgia Press, 1990), pp.1–36 (both reprinted in her *Form and Order*, above). British women's seals still await their historian.

SEALS OF THE SECULAR CLERGY

W.H. St John Hope, 'The Seals of English Bishops', *Proceedings of the Society of Antiquaries*, 2nd ser. 11 (1886–7), pp.271–306, gives a basic account of their development which has not been superseded. Other work on bishops' seals is restricted to a single see: [C.] Eyre, 'The Episcopal Seals of the Ancient Diocese of Glasgow', *Transactions of the Glasgow Archaeological Society*, 2nd ser. 2 (1896), pp.44–62; C.H. Hunter Blair, 'Medieval Seals of the Bishops of Durham', *Archaeologia*, 77 (1924), pp.1–24, which includes the bishops' palatinate seals; J.P. Dalton, *The Archiepiscopal and Deputed Seals of York 1114–1500* (Texts and Calendars no.17; York, Borthwick Institute of Historical Research, 1992). T.A. Heslop, 'The Episcopal Seals of Richard of Bury', in N. Coldstream and P. Draper (eds), *Medieval Art and Architecture at Durham Cathedral* (British Archaeological Association, Conference Transactions 3, 1980), pp.154–62, is important not only for its conclusions on the origins of these seals but also for its innovative analysis of their engraving.

On the lesser clergy's seals little has been written. W.H. St John Hope, 'The Seals of Archdeacons', *Proceedings of the Society of Antiquaries*, 2nd ser. 15 (1893–5), pp.26–35, is still the only general account. J.H. Bloom, 'Official Seals of the Diocese of Worcester', *Miscellanea Genealogica et Heraldica*, 5th ser. 4 (1920–2), pp.204–13, includes the seals of archdeacons, officials and peculiars as well as of the bishops. C.S. Perceval, 'Seals of Peculiar Jurisdictions', *Proceedings of the Society of Antiquaries*, 2nd ser. 5 (1870–3), pp.238–50, includes royal and manorial peculiars as well as those in clerical possession.

NON-HERALDIC PERSONAL SEALS

Despite their number, these are the least well catalogued or researched of all medieval seals. Except in Hunter Blair, 'Durham Seals', and Ellis, *Catalogue of Seals in the Public Record Office*, they are better represented in the catalogues of matrices than in the catalogues of impressions listed above. Preliminary investigations of these seals are in P.D.A. Harvey, 'Personal Seals in Thirteenth-Century England', in I. Wood and G.A. Loud (eds), *Church and Chronicle in the Middle Ages: Essays presented to John Taylor* (London, Hambledon Press, 1991), pp.117–27, and in A.F. McGuinness, 'Non-Armigerous Seals and Seal-Usage in Thirteenth-

Century England', *Thirteenth Century England*, vol.5 (Woodbridge, Boydell Press, 1995), pp.165–77. Jewish seals from England are described and illustrated in D.M. Friedenberg, *Medieval Jewish Seals from Europe* (Detroit, Wayne State University Press, 1987), pp.44–58. J.A. Goodall, 'The Earliest Imprese, a Study of some Medieval Seals and Devices', *Antiquaries Journal*, 73 (1993), pp.152–6, places them in the context of later Italian pictorial devices and mottoes. E.M. Elmhirst, *Merchants' Marks*, ed. L. Dow (Harleian Society, vol.108; 1959), illustrates a great range of these marks, many of them taken from seals.

SEALS OF RELIGIOUS HOUSES

The account of each house in the *Victoria History of the Counties of England* includes a note of its known seals, with some illustrations; the religious houses are mostly in the second or third volume for each county. G. Pedrick, *Monastic Seals of the XIIIth Century* (London, De La More Press, 1902), describes and illustrates some eighty seals of English houses. There are lists of the seals of the English Nation of the Hospitallers (covering the whole of the British Isles) in E.J. King, *The Seals of the Order of St John of Jerusalem* (London, Methuen and Co., 1932), pp.94–118, and of the English Province of the Franciscans (which included southern Scotland) in H.S. Kingsford, 'The Seals of the Franciscans', in A.G. Little (ed.), *Franciscan History and Legend in English Mediaeval Art* (British Society of Franciscan Studies, vol.19; Manchester, Manchester University Press, 1937), pp.81–100. Cistercian seals are discussed in D.H. Williams, 'The Seal in Cistercian Usage with Especial Reference to Wales', in B. Chauvin (ed.), *Mélanges à la Mémoire du Père Anselme Dimier* (Arbois, Benôit Chauvin, 6v., 1982–7), iii, pp.249–57, and T.A. Heslop, 'Cistercian Seals in England and Wales', in C. Norton and D. Park (eds), *Cistercian Art and Architecture in the British Isles*, (Cambridge, Cambridge University Press, 1986), pp.266–83, which includes as an appendix extracts from the order's legislation concerning seals. C. Clay, 'The Seals of the Religious Houses of Yorkshire', *Archaeologia*, 78 (1928), pp.1–36, is a full catalogue, with some discussion of the seals used by each order, and B. Kemp, 'The Seals of Reading Abbey', *Reading Medieval Studies*, 14 (1988), pp.139–62, is a valuable case-study of the seals used by one Benedictine monastery.

TOWN SEALS

W.H. St John Hope, 'The Municipal Seals of England and Wales', *Proceedings of the Society of Antiquaries*, 2nd ser. 15 (1894–5), pp.435–55, is a general account, and G. Pedrick, *Borough Seals of the Gothic Period* (London, J.M. Dent, 1904), describes and illustrates some seventy seals of English towns from the thirteenth century to the fifteenth. The emergence of town seals is discussed for England by J. Tait, *The Medieval English Borough* (Manchester, Manchester University Press, 1936), especially pp.235–9, and for Scotland by W.C. Dickinson (ed.), *Early Records of the Burgh of Aberdeen* (Scottish History Society, 3rd ser. 49; 1957), especially pp.xlix–li. Though concerned with French seals, B. Bedos-Rezak, 'Towns and Seals: Representation and Signification in Medieval France', *Bulletin of the John Rylands Library*, 72 (1990), pp.35–48 (reprinted in her *Form and Order*, above), says much that is relevant to town seals in Britain and to common seals in general. L. Jewitt and W.H. St John Hope, *The Corporation Plate and Insignia of Office of the Cities and Towns of England and Wales* (London, Bemrose and Sons Ltd, 2v., 1895), describe all and illustrate many of the matrices then in the possession of civic authorities. Accounts of the seals of particular towns include [C.] Eyre,'The Ancient Seal of the Burgh of Rutherglen', *Transactions of the Glasgow Archaeological Society*, 2nd ser. 2 (1896), pp.247–52; H. Lloyd Parry, *The Exeter Civic Seals* (Exeter, J.G. Commin, 1909); C.H. Hunter Blair, 'The Seals of Newcastle-upon-Tyne, *Archaeologia Aeliana*, 3rd ser. 19 (1922), pp.171–84; W.J. Hemp, 'The Town Seal of Haverfordwest', *Archaeologia Cambrensis*, 77 (1922), pp.383–9; and W. Smith, 'A Note on the Medieval Borough Seals of Wilton', *Journal of the Society of Archivists*, 8 (1986–7), pp.45–7. Statute Merchant seals are discussed and listed in C.S. Perceval, 'Seals under the Statute Merchant', *Proceedings of the Society of Antiquaries*, 2nd ser. 7 (1876–8), pp.107–19; 9 (1881–3), pp.253–61; and W.H. St John Hope, 'Seals of the Statute Merchant', *Proceedings of the Society of Antiquaries*, 2nd ser. 15 (1894–5), pp.61–6.

UNIVERSITY SEALS

W.H. St John Hope, 'Seals of the Colleges and of the University of Cambridge', *Proceedings of the Society of Antiquaries*, 2nd ser. 10 (1883–5), pp.225–52, includes a list of all he could trace. G.W. Campbell, 'The Seals of the University of Glasgow', *Transactions of the Glasgow Archaeological Society*, 2nd ser. 4 (1903), pp.65–74, includes interesting extracts from the university's records ordering its earliest seals to be made.

INDEX